I0450391

UKRAINE: MOVING BEYOND STALEMATE?

HEARING

BEFORE THE

COMMISSION ON SECURITY AND COOPERATION IN EUROPE

ONE HUNDRED ELEVENTH CONGRESS

SECOND SESSION

MARCH 16, 2010

Printed for the use of the
Commission on Security and Cooperation in Europe

[CSCE 111–2–3]

Available via http://www.csce.gov

U.S. GOVERNMENT PRINTING OFFICE

75–133 PDF   WASHINGTON : 2014

For sale by the Superintendent of Documents, U.S. Government Printing Office
Internet: bookstore.gpo.gov   Phone: toll free (866) 512–1800; DC area (202) 512–1800
Fax: (202) 512–2250   Mail: Stop SSOP, Washington, DC 20402–0001

COMMISSION ON SECURITY AND COOPERATION IN EUROPE

LEGISLATIVE BRANCH COMMISSIONERS

HOUSE

ALCEE L. HASTINGS, Florida,
  Co-Chairman
EDWARD J. MARKEY, Massachusetts
LOUISE McINTOSH SLAUGHTER,
  New York
MIKE McINTYRE, North Carolina
G.K. BUTTERFIELD, North Carolina
CHRISTOPHER H. SMITH, New Jersey
ROBERT B. ADERHOLT, Alabama
JOSEPH R. PITTS, Pennsylvania
DARRELL E. ISSA, California

SENATE

BENJAMIN L. CARDIN, Maryland,
  Chairman
CHRISTOPHER J. DODD, Connecticut
SHELDON WHITEHOUSE, Rhode Island
TOM UDALL, New Mexico
JEANNE SHAHEEN, New Hampshire
SAM BROWNBACK, Kansas
SAXBY CHAMBLISS, Georgia
RICHARD BURR, North Carolina
ROBERT F. WICKER, Mississippi

EXECUTIVE BRANCH COMMISSIONERS

Michael H. Posner, Department of State
Alexander Vershbow, Department of Defense
Michael C. Camuñez, Department of Commerce

(II)

UKRAINE: MOVING BEYOND STALEMATE?

MARCH 16, 2010

COMMISSIONERS

(III)

UKRAINE: MOVING BEYOND STALEMATE?

March 16, 2010

COMMISSION ON SECURITY AND COOPERATION IN EUROPE

WASHINGTON, DC

The hearing was held from 10 a.m. in room Senate Visitor Center 201/200, Washington, DC, Hon. Benjamin L. Cardin, Chairman, Commission on Security and Cooperation in Europe, presiding.

Commissioners present: Hon. Benjamin L. Cardin, Chairman, Commission on Security and Cooperation in Europe; and Hon. Alcee L. Hastings, Co-Chairman, Commission on Security and Cooperation in Europe.

Witnesses present: Daniel A. Russell, Deputy Assistant Secretary of State for Russia, Ukraine, Belarus and Moldova, Department of State; Damon Wilson, Vice President, Atlantic Council; and Anders Aslund, Senior Fellow, Peterson Institute for International Economics.

HON. BENJAMIN L. CARDIN, CHAIRMAN, COMMISSION ON SECURITY AND COOPERATION IN EUROPE

Mr. CARDIN. Well, good morning everyone and welcome to the hearing—the Helsinki Commission hearing on "Ukraine: Moving Beyond Stalemate?" I am pleased to welcome you to this hearing on Ukraine, an important partner for the United States and one of the largest countries in Europe, both in terms of size and population.

An independent, democratic and stable Ukraine is in America's interest and vital to the security of the OSCE region. Ukraine remains a country in transition, in part due to its tragic history. To visit, as I have, the memorials to Stalin's famine, Babi Yar and Chornobyl, is a stark reminder of the history of Ukraine.

Despite this legacy, especially since the 2004 Orange Revolution, there have been gains in political pluralism, media freedoms and holding of free and fair elections. Additionally, Ukraine is the only country among the 12 non-Baltic former Soviet states to earn the assessment of free by Freedom House.

The country has recently witnessed Presidential elections, which the OSCE assessed as having met international democratic standards. Ukraine faces a myriad challenges. Clearly, the President, along with the new Prime Minister and the Rada will need to accelerate economic and political reforms, tackle systematic corruption and overcome the rule of law deficits, including building up an underdeveloped judiciary.

(1)

Will Ukraine, despite tangible progress and freedom and democracy, be able to move beyond the stalemate that has stymied its ability to grapple with these difficult problems and slow this euro-Atlantic integration?

Nothing would be more important to strengthening Ukraine's independence and reducing its vulnerability to outside pressures, including strengthening its energy independence and bringing it closer to its stated European aspirations. Despite past disappointments, there is genuine desire in Washington that Ukraine succeed as an independent, democratic, stable and economically successful state.

Importantly, both the Congress and administration continue to strongly support the right of Ukraine to decide its own fate, consistent with the principles enshrined in the Helsinki Final Act. Today, we will examine Ukraine's future course following the February 7th elections, which the OSCE assessed as having met international democratic standards.

Our witnesses will focus on policy implications for the United States, examining how the U.S. can best continue to encourage and assist Ukraine in the development of democracy, rule of law and market economy at home as well as relationships with its neighbors, the United States and the European institutions. And we look forward to hearing from our distinguished panel of witnesses.

For our first panel, I'm pleased to have with us today, Mr. Daniel Russell, Deputy Assistant Secretary of State for Russia, Ukraine, Belarus and Moldova. Since joining the Foreign Service in 1983, Mr. Russell has held a variety of positions in Washington and abroad, most recently, as Chief of Staff to Undersecretary of State for Political Affairs Bill Burns. And prior to that, the Deputy Chief of Mission in Moscow, Russia and Kazakhstan. Mr. Russell, it's a pleasure to have you before the Commission.

DANIEL A. RUSSELL, DEPUTY ASSISTANT SECRETARY OF STATE FOR RUSSIA, UKRAINE, BELARUS AND MOLDOVA, DEPARTMENT OF STATE

Mr. RUSSELL. Thank you very much, Mr. Chairman. I will apologize in advance for my voice. It's part of the burden of having two young children. But look, thank you very much for your invitation to discuss Ukraine and its relations with the United States in the wake of Presidential elections. Your timing could not be better.

Let me begin by making three basic points about Ukraine and the recent elections before sketching out our agenda for engagement. My first point should be obvious. Ukraine matters. Ukraine matters to the United States. Ukraine matters to Europe. Ukraine has tremendous potential. It could become a net contributor to global food security.

It could become self-sufficient in energy. Ukraine can also serve as an example in a critical region. It has shown leadership on the world stage, giving up its nuclear weapons to become a non-nuclear state and contributing to peacekeeping operations from the Balkans to Iraq. Ukraine serves—also serves as a transit route through which nearly a quarter of Europe's gas flows.

My second point is about Ukraine's leadership in democracy in the region. Taken together, the conduct of its Presidential elections received an overwhelmingly positive assessment from international observers. I should add that among those observers were Congressman Hastings and staff of your Commission and I would like to commend their contribution.

The OSCE concluded that the Presidential elections showed significant progress over previous elections and met most OSCE and Council of Europe standards. The open competitive election demonstrated respect for civil and political rights and offered voters a genuine choice.

My third point is about the 2010 election—how we look at it. It may have been a defeat for the Orange Revolution leaders, but it's far from a defeat for the Orange Revolution. Elections should be viewed, I think, as another step in strengthening Ukraine's democracy and Ukrainians should take pride in what they've achieved.

The post-election transfer of power has been orderly. Prime Minister Tymoshenko initially challenged the results in court, but withdrew her case. When formation of a political parliamentary majority coalition appeared unlikely, President Yanukovych and his Party of Regions sought and won passage of a new law that allows coalition formation, not only with political parties, but with independent deputies.

On that basis, Prime Minister Azarov and his Cabinet were confirmed last week. The opposition questioned the new laws' constitutionality and we were pleased to see that the Party of Regions itself took the initiative to ask the constitutional court to review the law and pledge to abide by its decision.

With the election now behind him, President Yanukovych faces the challenge of governing. Obviously, he and his new team need some time to organize themselves, but I think some key elements of his approach are obvious. Economic recovery will rightly be his top priority and he has inherited a difficult situation at a difficult moment.

With regard to foreign policy, I think President Yanukovych has been quite clear. He wants to continue Ukraine's strategic partnership with the United States. He wants to improve relations with Russia and he wants to pursue integration with the European Union.

And as we look ahead to engagement with President Yanukovych and his new team, it's, I think, worth reviewing the underlying premises of U.S. policy toward Ukraine. Simply put, the United States will not waver in its support for a strong and independent Ukraine. We want to see, as you mention, Ukraine succeed.

Our vision for Ukraine, I think, is the vision that most Ukrainians want, a democratic and prosperous European nation with an effective and accountable government. Charting the course for Ukraine is of course, a decision to be made by Ukrainians and their elected leaders. There has been speculation over the past year that the Obama administration's efforts to improve relations with Russia would somehow threaten our relationship with Ukraine.

I think that was not correct and it is not correct. As we reset relations with Russia, we have reaffirmed our commitment to the sovereignty and territorial integrity of Ukraine and its neighbors. We do not believe that a partnership with one country comes at the expense of another.

The stronger our partners, the more effective our partnerships. I would posit that a strong and independent Ukraine is good for Russia, good for the region and good for the world. There's also been speculation about Ukraine's relationship with NATO during a Yanukovych Presidency. Let me be clear that the United States continues to support Ukraine's deepening ties to NATO and to the European Union.

But again, these are decisions to be made by Ukrainians and their leaders. We recognize that how far and how fast to proceed will be a Ukrainian choice. President Yanukovych has said that he wishes to continue programs of cooperation with NATO at existing levels but NATO membership is not on his agenda. We respect that choice. But we want the Ukrainians to know that NATO's door remains open.

We look forward to cooperating with Ukraine to meet its objectives in the NATO-Ukraine Commission and its Annual National Programme. Because of the importance that we attach to our relationship with Ukraine, once the Central Election Commission had announced the full electronic results of the election, President Obama was among the first world leaders to congratulate Viktor Yanukovych on his victory.

National Security Advisor General Jones led the U.S. delegation at the Presidential Inauguration, where he met not only President Yanukovych, but Prime Minister Tymoshenko. And Mrs. Tymoshenko is obviously going to be one of the leaders in the opposition in parliament and we are going to continue our longstanding relationship with her.

At the same time, we also plan to work closely with emerging leaders like Deputy Prime Minister Tigipko and Member of Parliament Arseniy Yatseniuk. The development of new democratic leaders is important for all parties in Ukraine. Let me underscore that U.S. policy toward Ukraine will continue to focus on strengthening our strategic partnership.

Our engagement and cooperation with Ukraine will continue to be guided by the U.S.-Ukraine Charter on Strategic Partnership. The charter outlines enhanced cooperation across the full spectrum of mutual priorities, including economics, trade and energy, defense and security, strengthening democracy and people-to-people and cultural exchanges.

To advance the objectives of that charter, we now have a strategic partnership commission, established during the Vice President's visit to Kyiv last July. Our commitment to Ukraine is also evidenced by our assistance program—$123 million this year. The goals of our assistance are to bolster peace and security, strengthen democratic institutions, promote economic growth and energy efficiency, enhance security, secure Chornobyl, fight AIDS and HIV and improve child health.

In the spirit of our strategic partnership with Ukraine, I'd like to suggest five policy priorities that should be high on our shared agenda with the Yanukovych Presidency. First, the United States is committed to policies that contribute to a democratic and prosperous Ukraine. And the United States stands ready to help Ukraine reach agreement with the International Monetary Fund as soon as possible.

The path to economic recovery and renewed prosperity runs through agreement with the IMF, which can help provide Ukraine a way out of the current crisis and open the door to lending for other—from other international financial institutions in the European Union. That will require resolute leadership and hard decisions to undertake the critical reforms needed to fix the budget deficit, revive the banking sector and phaseout energy subsidies.

A second, and I would say equally important, policy area for Ukraine's long-term prosperity and economic independence is energy-sector reform. A gas sector based on transparency, competition, realistic pricing and more energy-efficient gas distribution and consumption will be key.

Third, the United States is ready to work to strengthen the business side of Ukraine—U.S.-Ukraine relations, which frankly, I think, are weaker than they should be. We welcome President Yanukovych's remarks in favor of creating incentives for investors such as lowering taxes and cutting red tape.

Our business community tells us that there is much more to be done to make Ukraine attractive to investors, from greater rule of law protection to serious action against corruption. The payment of VAT—V–A–T—refunds would be a big step forward, I think, and a sign to our investors.

A fourth area of cooperation in our relationship with Ukraine lies in nuclear security. We look forward to building on our successful record of nonproliferation with Ukraine at the upcoming nuclear security summit here and we look forward to President Yanukovych attending. Thanks to the leadership of Sen. Lugar and former Sen. Nunn, we can point to vital cooperation between Ukraine and the United States that has made the world safer.

Finally, the United States wishes to strengthen bilateral security and defense cooperation. As part of that effort, we hope that the Ukrainian parliament will pass legislation to allow joint military exercises on its territory this year. While the challenges in U.S.-Ukrainian relations are complex and demanding, I remain optimistic about the possibilities before us.

It's important to both nations and both peoples to get this relationship right. We have a chance at the beginning of a new Presidency in Kyiv to redouble our efforts to do so. And I hope that both Ukrainians and Americans both inside and outside of government will take advantage of that opportunity.

Thank you very much and I'm happy to answer your questions.

Mr. CARDIN. Well, Mr. Russell, thank you very much for your testimony. We've been joined by the House Chair of the Helsinki Commission Alcee Hastings. As you've already pointed out, Mr. Hastings was present as an observer in the elections in Ukraine and helped in the certification of Mr. Yanukovych's elections. So we thank our House Chair for his active involvement and the ability to give us a first-hand report as to the progress of democracy in Ukraine.

I want to, I guess, ask you a fundamental question first and then I'll turn it to my Co-Chair. You talk about Mr. Yanukovych's desire to strengthen the ties with the West and the East about developing stronger ties, certainly, with Russia, but also with the United States and Europe. And then you talk about our NATO desires, that we still believe that this is a country that is important in our European security arrangements.

How can he accomplish all that? How can he strengthen the tie between Ukraine and Russia, which was stressed during the Orange Revolution and which Mr. Yanukovych was not a supporter of? Now, he's all of a sudden going to be able to maintain this development with the West, with Europe and with Russia and also perhaps be with us in NATO. How does he balance all that? It seems like that's an impossible task.

Mr. RUSSELL. Well, we're going to see how good he is at it. I think it was interesting that he chose to make his first trip abroad to Brussels. He talked about European integration and a free trade agreement with the EU. Then, to go to Moscow and create—finish the leg of his triad by coming here for the nuclear assistance security summit.

So he clearly is going to try to balance these three interests. And I don't think it's a bad idea, actually. I mean nobody's going to move in their neighborhood. Russia's not going to go away. Russia's Ukraine's second largest trading partner after the European Union. And I think he's got a good shot at making some progress on all of this. But like I said, we're going to be there pushing for strategic partnership.

Mr. CARDIN. Well, how much influence will Russia have in the priorities that he places on the agenda for security?

Mr. RUSSELL. It's an open book. He's just named his government, so we're going to have to see. I mean he's trying to be all things to all people like many leaders. We'll see if he succeeds.

Mr. CARDIN. Well, let me ask you just one more question on a subject that the Orange Revolution was not successful in dealing with and it's corruption. It's been a—we've seen first-hand the consequences of corruption within Ukraine. It's not unique for countries in transition, but certainly, the game plan to deal with it has not been as successful as the United States would like to see it. Do you have any view as to how this new government will deal with the problems the country faces in corruption?

Mr. RUSSELL. Well, we agree with your assessment. It is a major problem in practically, every field. Our human rights report, which we just put out talks again about corruption, which everybody knows. And I think it's going to be key. If he's going to make progress on economic recovery, he's got to deal with this because, if he's going to get ahead on economic recovery, he's really got to start with sound fiscal policies and pass the budget.

He's got to figure out how to get the private sector to really fuel economic recovery and they need an effective banking sector to provide the financing to do that. Well, if you don't deal with corruption, you're just not going to get—you're not going to get investors. And transparency and rule of law are part of the keys. He's talked about this and we're going to have to see how they do, but I agree, it should be a priority and it's something the United States is going to push.

Mr. CARDIN. I'll look at your five issues that you've raised for priorities. Certainly, democracy and prosperity is going to depend upon dealing with the corruption issues, the energy sector reforms, very much so and we push the EITI as a framework to deal with the energy sector issues.

On business, business and investment by the United States or any country in Ukraine will be very much dependent upon a comfort level as it relates to dealing with the issues of corruption. So on every one of these areas, it's going to be fundamental that they have to deal with this and their track record's not very good.

Mr. RUSSELL. I agree with you. I think they'll probably have a new program with the IMF and I suspect that transparency and rule of law are going to be a big part of that. I should also mention that we're coordinating with the European Union because I think if he wants to pursue European integration, clearly all of these issues are going to be key to that as well because the European Union's goals for integration are not particularly different than our own bilateral goals in this respect.

Mr. CARDIN. So what is your advice to Congress? What would be your top recommendations for what the Congress should do in order to reinforce the goals that you laid out—with your goals that we fully support and we certainly encourage the new government to improve relations with all of its neighbors. That is fundamental to your regional stability and it's fundamental to U.S. interests. What would your advice be to Congress?

Mr. RUSSELL. Well, I think, your Co-Chairman here has set a good example for engagement early on with Ukraine and I think it's important. I think it's important that the Congress is dealing—this is a country where the Rada, their parliament is very important, that you engage with the leadership there as we're doing in the executive branch to try to push that forward.

And we're going to look for your support, obviously, with our assistance programs. And if, you can encourage some of the private-sector businesses in your states that if Ukraine does make some of these changes, to try to look and see if investment there or business opportunities would be a possibility.

Mr. CARDIN. Well, as I said in my opening statement, Ukraine is very important to U.S. interests. It's a high priority of our Commission. We have spent a lot of time visiting Ukraine because we thought it was important to do that on many occasions and so clearly, it's just going to be a continued focal point for our interest because we think it's important to the entire OSCE region.

With that, let me turn to Congressman Hastings and again, thank him for his leadership on the traveling to Ukraine and in his continued leadership on this country and the place that the Helsinki Commission has placed in following the events in Ukraine.

HON. ALCEE L. HASTINGS, CO-CHAIRMAN, COMMISSION ON SECURITY AND COOPERATION IN EUROPE

Mr. HASTINGS. Thank you very much, Mr. Chair. OK, it's on. And Mr. Russell, thank you very much. Mr. Chairman, I'm sure it's already been noted—my humble apologies for being delayed. I had the distinct privilege and honor to participate in three Ukrainian elections, including the first round of the just-passed Presidential elections.

In addition to just being an election observer, I also like to consider myself a good observer of people. And while I don't speak the language, on two different occasions in Ukraine, one during the Orange Revolution and on the very last visit, I took it upon myself to walk into areas, first, during the Orange Revolution that I had not been in and a second time, to go back into those again.

And then of course, as you might know, Mr. Russell, a considerable number of Ukrainians in the diaspora and those in academia and the think tanks and in government all talk to us a great deal about Ukraine. One thing, if I had to characterize the residual from the Orange Revolution, it would be unfilled promises. That would just be all that I would say.

The other things that I note is considerable frustration among those that are supporters of the efforts that have been put forward in Ukraine. Now, the United States doesn't have to make any apologies to anybody and I'm not suggesting that they ever would, but we have a solid record of standing with the Ukrainian people over the decades in support of their struggle for freedom and democracy.

I'll start by asking you how you assess the Prime Minister's remarks last week and I'm paraphrasing what he said, that their treasury is depleted. I'm reminded—that's very similar to our nation at this time, a President, inheriting some 30 years of transformation of an economy, is expected in 1 year to reverse it.

Mr. Yanukovych and his new coalition, in my judgment, have a very high hill to hustle and they cannot do it, quite frankly, without the United States and Russia and the European Union and with some clear understanding of how the international community that is experiencing a global crisis of its own is going to be able to address it. So I guess I'd like to know from you the status of Ukraine with respect to the Millennium Challenge Account.

Mr. RUSSELL. Well, the Millennium Challenge Account threshold program didn't succeed. I mean, the Millennium Challenge Corporation chose not to continue it in 2009 because of Ukraine's performance. And I can't say where they'll go from here. Corruption was one of the big issues, actually.

But to the broader point that you're making, which I agree with, they've got a tough row to hoe. But I think that they've got to try to reach agreement with the IMF has to be the first priority because that's what's going to unlock the doors to the other lending they need to survive.

In the longer term, I mean, the shorter your time horizon with Ukraine, the more pessimistic you're going to be. The more you stretch that out, the more optimistic. I mean they have gas reserves. They have oil; they have a lot of coal. Their manufacturing sector actually did pretty well before the economic recession.

I think they've got to go back to basics. And frankly Anders Åslund—it's always very difficult to talk about economics when you have, actually, a real economist sitting behind you—[laughter]—he can probably help you more than me with most of this.

Mr. HASTINGS. All right. Looking ahead, in 2017, the lease agreement with Russia in the Black Sea are going to become more and more an issue. Attendant to that is the fact that we, the United States, really have poured millions of dollars and security assistance cooperation to Ukraine and yet, it seems their armed forces are still in need of reform and modernization.

So I guess, do we still look to try and bring them into NATO? What's your take on the Black Sea as it pertains to Mr. Yanukovych? And what are the substantive benefits of our security cooperation with Ukraine beyond just building our relationships?

Mr. RUSSELL. Well, I think that defense and security cooperation is a key part of our relationship. I think you're right that there's a lot more to be done, but at the same time, I mean, this is a country where you now have civilian control of the military. You have an all-volunteer officer corps. They've made some key reforms that they've got more to do.

I know our own military finds them very enthusiastic and good to work with and they have an interest and we have an interest in seeing them become a net contributor to global security. They still have a pretty good-sized presence among peacekeepers in Kosovo.

They've contributed to Iraq and Afghanistan and other U.N. peacekeeping missions and NATO missions and I think that's what's in it for us in the longer term. The question you posed about the Black Sea fleet; I don't know what they're going to do, but what we support is Ukraine's independence and territorial integrity and their right to make their own foreign policy choices. So whatever they do, we would support something that obviously, they freely enter into.

Mr. HASTINGS. The last couple of questions that I have deal specifically with what your sentiments are at this time and what the administration, if anything, is picking up—if anything—regarding Kyiv's desire to have a Euro-Atlantic integration. Is that still viable? I heard you say that the new President's first visit was to Brussels, but I hasten to add that his second visit was to Moscow. And so where they'll go with—[laughter]—Ukraine at this point?

Mr. RUSSELL. Well, I think our approach as far as NATO is that Mr. Yanukovych has said he wants to continue practical cooperation. There's a lot that needs to be done, and can be done through the NATO-Ukraine Commission, through the Annual National Programme they have with NATO and all these good things for a more modern, more professional military and defense establishment. And I think they're worth continuing no matter what they choose to do on the larger question of NATO membership.

I think with European integration, it's pretty clear that Mr. Yanukovych has already talked about a free trade agreement with the European Union and liberalization of their visa regime. And again, all of that's going to require some changes we've been talking about toward meeting European Union standards.

I think there's—in some ways, not much choice. I mean, they want to become a modern, prosperous nation and that will require being part of the international community in a different way than they were in the past century.

Mr. HASTINGS. Well, you have a rather considerable portfolio, but as it pertains to Ukraine, two of the neighbors that are also in your portfolio, Belarus and Moldova—I'll leave Russia to the side because I know that's overarching. But just as it pertains to Belarus and Moldova, what do you see for the future of Ukraine relations with those two countries?

Mr. RUSSELL. Well, I mean, we hope to see a good relationship in Ukrainian bilateral relations with both of those countries. Moldova has had quite a change in its own government, bringing in a new coalition that's committed to European integration as its foreign policy and to rule of law and democracy at home, which we see is a very, very good and welcome development.

Ukraine can help to support that. There's some basic issues about delineation of the border between the part of Moldova that is Transnistria and Ukraine—Ukraine also plays a role in the five-plus-two talks looking at a settlement to this longstanding frozen conflict. So they can do quite a bit there.

Ukraine's always had a reasonably good relationship with Belarus. As you know, the United States—Mr. Cardin knows from his recent trip there—we have some real issues in our own relationship with them and we would hope that Ukraine's relationship would help to push toward a more open system there and make some small steps toward a more open, pluralistic government.

Mr. HASTINGS. Right. Well, finally, Mr. Chairman, time won't permit us to explore the importance of Poland in all of this as well, so I'll just leave that to the side. But let me offer what I think are two things that help in our developing better and building better relationships with countries.

And it's not ignored, but not enough emphasis is placed on cultural and educational exchanges. And as policymakers, Senator Cardin, my dear friend and Co-Chair of this Commission and I have been active in pursuing funding in that arena. But I believe Ukraine would benefit greatly by large student exchanges and cultural exchanges. They have so much to offer and in that regard, it would be helpful if we were to participate.

Now, let me be a little more precise and I'll stop right here. If I had to make a bet on where 19- and 20-year-olds are going to go to college, that can with the support of their families or however they manage to do so, I'll bet you Russia is going to do more in the education arena having them come to Russia than we are having them come to America. I'll stop right there.

Mr. CARDIN. Well, Congressman Hastings, thank you very much for those observations. I would just observe I think the two greatest challenges will be for Ukraine as to whether it really can establish itself as an independent democracy in that region, which is our goal and being able to establish relations with all of its neighbors, including to the West. And second, whether it can deal with corruption.

We've mentioned this a couple times, and the Millennium Challenge grant is a good example. We just completed a hearing in the Senate Foreign Relations Committee with President Clinton and Bill Gates who are involved in two major foundations that provide international assistance. And I was very impressed with their commitment on accountability in making sure the funds do not get sidetracked to help finance corrupt activities.

We are looking at a change in our foreign assistance programs and accountability's going to be part of that. So Ukraine is a developing democracy that is—needs an independent economy and they will have an independent economy, but it will not happen at the pace that they want if they can't get corruption under control.

So I think those two issues are critically important as we watch Ukraine. And I agree with Congressman Hastings. We need to look at its relationship with other countries; whether Moldova or Belarus, Ukraine can play a very important role in the development of other countries in transition in that region.

So I think it's in all of our interests to continue our focus on Ukraine and just observe with a great deal of, I think, optimism, the recent elections being the expression the people of Ukraine as to the future of their country. And we certainly are impressed by the new government's ability to form under very challenging circumstances. Thank you, Mr. Russell, for your testimony.

Mr. RUSSELL. Thank you.

Mr. HASTINGS. Thank you, Mr. Russell.

Mr. CARDIN. I would want to observe that the Ambassador for Ukraine had planned to be with us. He has taken ill. He must have similar children that you have. [Laughter.] And maybe more in number, so he's maybe more severely impacted. We're very pleased to have two distinguished experts on Ukraine for our second panel.

Damon Wilson is Vice President, Director of International Security Programs at the Atlantic Council. Mr. Wilson previously served as Special Assistant to the President and Senior Director of European Affairs at NSC. We're among his many responsibilities. He coordinated interagency policy in support of Ukraine, including during the Orange Revolution. Mr. Wilson also served in a variety of other governmental positions at NSC and State Department including as Chief of Staff at the U.S. Embassy in Iraq.

Anders Aslund is Senior Fellow at the Peterson Institute for International Economics and has been deeply engaged with Ukraine since 1985. Previously, Dr. Aslund was Director of the Russian and Eurasia Program at the Carnegie Endowment and is the author of nine books, including "How Ukraine Became a Market Economy and Democracy." And he has a copy here, willing to sell it, I assume. [Laughter.] We have extra copies that we'll make available.

Mr. ASLUND. Free copy.

Mr. CARDIN. Thank you. We'll start off with Mr. Wilson.

Mr. WILSON. Thank you very much, Mr. Chairman, Mr. Co-Chairman.

Mr. HASTINGS. Press that button, Damon. See if it's on.

DAMON WILSON, VICE PRESIDENT, ATLANTIC COUNCIL

Mr. WILSON. Oh yes, thank you. Thank you, again. I'm honored to speak to you today about our relationship with Ukraine. I want to thank the Commission for the role that it's taken in helping to raise the spotlight in Washington on the issue.

Mr. HASTINGS. I apologize to you, but some of the people in the back are still having difficulty hearing. Is that red light on, on that mic?

Mr. WILSON. It's hard to see. Yes.

Mr. HASTINGS. All right. There, you're better now.

Mr. WILSON. All right, is that better?

Mr. HASTINGS. Yeah.

Mr. WILSON. All right. I want to thank you, again.

Mr. CARDIN. That's three thank-you's. [Laughter.]

Mr. WILSON. Naturally. But I did want to thank the Commission for taking the opportunity to help raise the attention—the spotlight on Ukraine here in Washington. I think that's an important function of the Commission and I applaud that leadership. I also want to thank you, Mr. Co-Chairman, for your personal leadership and the role that you've played in elections in Ukraine over the years. I think that's been very important. I commend my former colleague, Dan Russell, for some excellent testimony.

Today, I'd like to underscore why the issue of Ukraine should matter in Washington, outlining key benchmarks against which to judge the policies of Ukraine's new President and offer recommendations for U.S. policy. I agree that we should not underestimate what has just happened in Ukraine this year.

This election is a victory for the consolidation of democracy. And yet for most of us that follow Ukraine closely, there is a sense of disappointment. Why is that? First, the leaders of the Orange Revolution failed to deliver for Ukraine that which those protestors on the Maidan were calling for back in 2004.

Second, Ukraine's track record of good elections has yet to translate into a track record of good governance. And third, we've been disappointed by the timidity in the West to continue to support Ukraine. So President Yanukovych, therefore, assumes the Presidency in an atmosphere of pragmatism.

And a sober assessment of Ukraine's prospects is appropriate. However, the vision of a democratic, free-market Ukraine firmly anchored in Europe remains important as it remains a motivator for tough policy decisions in Kyiv as well as in Brussels and Washington. And we must not take this vision for granted.

Why does all of this matter? First, it matters for the quality of life of Ukrainian citizens, but it also matters geopolitically. In some sense, Ukraine is untethered, if you will. Its future is not certain. Although it is an ancient nation, it is a young state. The history of conflict in Europe is about uncertainty in the space between Germany and Russia.

And this would not matter if the Russia of today had evolved and changed to become like the Germany of today. But Russia has not. Ukraine's statehood remains fragile. If Ukrainian democracy continues to succeed and helps produce good governance and economic growth, it will serve as a powerful example in a region that desperately needs positive examples.

And that is why Russia has a strategy, which in some terms essentially is rollback. This strategy had been well articulated by Russia's leaders, including President Medvedev's declaration of privileged interests—the commitment to protect Russian citizens wherever they may live—as well as in Russia's new security strategy. In contrast, I'm not convinced that either the West or Ukraine itself has a very clear strategy about the way forward.

So let me first address Ukrainian policy, as what President Yanukovych does will have more of an impact on Ukraine's place in the world than any outside actor. He's off to a good start with an early visit to Brussels followed by one to Moscow. He's outlined his four top priorities of EU integration, returning good neighborly relations with Russia, developing relations with Ukraine's neighbors and pursuing strategic partnership with the United States. I think as we look forward, we should judge Ukrainian policy by several benchmarks.

First, Russia—how does Kyiv manage its relationships with Moscow? A stable and positive bilateral dynamic requires Ukraine to behave as and be treated as a sovereign, independent actor. Key issues include whether Yanukovych maintains a non-recognition policy toward South Ossetia and Abkhazia and whether he opens the door to an extension on the Black Sea fleet in Sevastopol.

Energy security—Russian interests have been keen to gain control of Ukraine's energy structure. Will Yanukovych agree? If he believes energy is a national security issue as I do, the new government would pursue a serious energy efficiency strategy.

International economics—The government's handling of the IMF will be an early test of its credibility. I'll leave the details of this to Anders, but similarly, a key question is how Yanukovych handles the common economic space with Russia? Does he do so in a way that negatively impacts Ukraine's WTO membership or the prospects for a free trade agreement with the EU?

Regional relations—Does Ukraine use its regional weight to support Moldova and a resolution of Transnistria? How Yanukovych handles ties with Belarusian leader Lukashenka and Georgian President Saakashvili will offer insights into the regional role that Ukraine will play, as well as the role that it wants to assume within Guam.

The European Union—Will Yanukovych press as hard to grow Ukraine's bilateral ties with the EU, as well as take advantage of the Eastern Partnership? A free trade agreement and visa liberalization are key practical steps which would help Ukrainians actually be Europeans and move the country toward Europe.

Nonproliferation—Ukraine had a spotty record of nonproliferation under then-Prime Minister Yanukovych. Will Ukraine's arms sales track record continue to improve given the economic interests at stake?

And finally NATO—NATO is clearly not at the top of the agenda, nor should it be. But NATO-Ukraine relations do need to be on the agenda. Yanukovych, in fact, had a track record as Prime Minister of advancing NATO-Ukraine ties. So while the window has closed on rapid movement toward NATO, both sides should ensure that there is substance to underpin the NATO-Ukraine Commission. As NATO is a demand-driven bureaucracy, the signals from Kyiv will determine the substance.

I believe it is an imperative to maintain the credibility of the historic Bucharest summit decision that Ukraine will become a member of the alliance. If we look back in 5 to 10 years and the Bucharest decision is seen as hollow, there will be damaging implications for the alliance's credibility, as well as for Ukraine.

In the face of Russian opposition and genuine divisions within Ukraine, some have argued that we should aim for Finlandization of Ukraine—independent, but not part of any alliance. When applied to Ukraine, these analysts imply that big powers taking decisions about Ukraine's future—I believe Ukraine must be in a position to determine its own future, including whether to pursue any membership in any alliance.

These issues provide benchmarks against which we can judge the new government. I have modest expectations, but do believe that Yanukovych can deliver on his campaign pledge to move—continuing moving Ukraine toward Europe. His early visit to Brussels and his reception in Brussels are good signs.

Yet the most important factor to achieve this foreign policy goal is what the government does domestically. Yanukovych's reception in Western capitals will be determined by whether he governs effectively, protects democratic advances, stabilizes and grows the economy and ensures Ukraine is a reliable energy partner.

In terms of implications for U.S. policy, I'm not convinced that the West as a unit yet has a coherent strategy, although Vice President Biden's visit to Kyiv last year helped lay out excellent principles for U.S. policy. We cannot afford to put Ukraine on the backburner or accept the argument that U.S. engagement is somehow provocative to Moscow. We should not accept the argument that Ukraine is messy or too divided as an excuse to not engage.

While changes in Ukraine are unlikely to be decisive in the next few years, the trend lines could take Ukraine further away from rather than closer to Europe. And we do not want to look back at Ukraine's next election and wonder what happened. So Mr. Chairman, as part of my effort to outline a way ahead for U.S. policy toward Ukraine, I offer six recommendations to conclude.

First, be in the game. Ukraine is in play and we need to engage and be present. The appointment of John Tefft as our Ambassador and the visits by Vice President Biden, National Security Advisor Jones and President Obama's congratulatory call to Yanukovych are key steps in this effort. This high-level outreach should continue.

Second, articulate a vision. We need to recommit to building a Europe whole and free, energizing the bipartisan tradition behind this vision and making clear that Ukraine has a place within this vision, as does Russia.

Third, maintain funding. We need to protect our funding for transition in Ukraine, as the Freedom Support Act model of graduation no longer applies in Europe's East in my view. Higher per capita GDP does not necessarily translate into a democratic Ukraine anchored firmly in Europe.

Fourth, reach beyond leaders. Unfortunately, Yushchenko was a failure. Yanukovych is unlikely to bring decisive change. We therefore need to ensure that our relations with Ukraine extend beyond leaders. We should place emphasis on developing next-generation leaders, ties with the Rada, engaging the regions and fostering people-to-people ties.

Fifth, push energy efficiency. The United States and Ukraine need to get serious about working with European partners to support energy efficiency in Ukraine as a national security strategy.

And sixth, enhance military-to-military ties. We must ensure that close military-to-military ties continue and are backed with funding from foreign military financing and foreign military sales and we must push back when Russia tries to portray military cooperation with Ukraine as provocative.

In the wake of Ukraine's election, Yanukovych is now President and his party leads the government. Now is the time to move beyond stalemate. Just as much as we hold Kyiv to that standard, we must hold ourselves to that standard. Thank you, Mr. Chairman, Mr. Co-Chairman. I look forward to your questions.

Mr. CARDIN. Mr. Wilson, thank you for your comments. Dr. Åslund?

ANDERS ÅSLUND, SENIOR FELLOW, PETERSON INSTITUTE FOR INTERNATIONAL ECONOMICS

Mr. ÅSLUND. Thank you very much, Mr. Chairman. And I would very much like to thank you for this opportunity to speak on a topic that I consider very important: how Ukraine should move beyond the stalemate—as you so rightly have put it in the headline—in the sphere of economic reform. I leave the political aspects to Dan Russell and Damon Wilson and just want to concur with their statement and I'll focus entirely upon the economic aspects.

Ukraine has established an open market economy with predominant private ownership. And from 2000 to 2007, the country had an average economic growth of 7.5 percent a year. But then came the global financial crisis and last year, GDP fell by no less than 15 percent. And this shows partly that Ukraine is part of the world economy but it also shows that it's not performing up to its potential. Its big problems, as you pointed out, Mr. Chairman, is pervasive corruption and poor business environment. And the question today is what and how can be done about it?

I co-chaired an independent international expert commission that has done a report on what the new government should do during its first year in power. We call it, "Proposals for Ukraine 2010: Time for Reforms." And our contention is that Ukraine today has a unique possibility to move ahead because a new Presidential election with a new government is always a good time to take reform. And on top of that, if you have been badly beaten by an economic crisis and are coming out of it, then you can act.

And our three main conclusions to put it first is that Ukraine needs a new capacity for economic reform. Second, a clear prioritization of what the top priorities are so that they are really carried out. And third, it needs to utilize international organizations as lighthouses or anchors to guide its reforms.

So let me start with the first point. Ukraine needs to establish a new capacity that is independent of the agencies to be reformed. We recommended the creation of the reform commission at the cabinet of ministers headed by a powerful Deputy Prime Minister, such as Deputy Prime Minister Sergei Tigipko has now been appointed. The reform commission should have its own budget and a single goal to decide and implement reform. This must come from above.

At the same time, President Yanukovych has now formed a reform committee at the Presidential administration that he chairs himself. And he did set this up on the second day of—his second day in office. And he has also appointed the first deputy head of his Presidential administration, Iryna Akimova, who's an outstanding economic reformer, to be the executive secretary of his reform.

Second point is that Ukraine needs to have clear reform priorities. And the short of it is that they must improve the effectiveness of a state, achieve financial stability, allow private enterprise, the freedom of the market and make social policy more effective.

And the government has adopted a coalition program that is already out which is called "Stability and Reform." By and large, all the bullet points in this program are the right ones. But of course, they are bullet points rather than clear plans. So this looks promising. And it—to a considerable extent—it reflects the views of our Commission.

The problem in Ukraine so far has not been what should be done. There's a broad public consensus. The question is if it should be done and who should do it. There's always a reason not to do things.

And therefore we think that as everybody here has expressed today, the United States, the IMF and other international organizations need to help Ukraine to break through this political logjam, which is very much created by the interests of corruption. And naturally the United States should engage in the promotion of reforms that are beneficial for Ukraine's future governance and economic welfare.

To summarize our Commission report, we've found 10 top priorities for this year: First, carry out gas reform. That's vital. Second, make the national bank of Ukraine independent to give a proper basis for the banking system. Third, move toward inflation targeting with a floating exchange rate to stop future high inflation. Fourth, cut public expenditures. There's no way to run a country with a budget deficit of 8 to 10 percent of GDP in budget deficit.

Fifth, undertake comprehensive deregulation of enterprise capital—this red tape. Sixth, conclude a European association agreement, which would include a deep and comprehensive free trade agreement. Seven, get privatization going again. Eight, legalize private sales of agriculture land. Nine, adopt a law of the public information to fight corruption. And 10, complete the modern commercial legislation.

And all these measures are truly vital and they can be implemented within a year. In most cases, they're already draft laws lying ready to be adopted. And if I should pick a—point out one thing that is absolutely key, that's the gas reform. Currently Ukraine subsidizes the import of Russian gas to the tune of 3 percent of GDP each year, which makes no sense whatsoever. And this has to be changed.

As Dan Russell in particular pointed out, the IMF will be the key in this process. The IMF will go out and start negotiating a new agreement very soon indeed. And it will contain a gas reform and sensible macroeconomic polices. And of course, the European Union is also currently negotiating a substantial association agreement and it is also involved in the gas reform.

The role of the United States here as the biggest shareholder in the IMF is, of course, push the IMF in action as Dan Russell spoke about. And the U.S. also should engage in the gas reform. I think that Congressman Hastings mentioned something very important. Ukraine needs a new, broader educated elite. And therefore, I think that the United States should offer hundreds of student scholarships for Ukrainian scholars to come to this country. Let me thank you with these words.

Mr. CARDIN. Well, let me thank both of you for your testimony. It was very specific on benchmarks and recommendations. I think that's very helpful to us, but I hope it's helpful also to Ukraine. I think that your lists there, particularly on benchmarks, Mr. Wilson, and recommendations, Dr. Åslund, were both very helpful to us.

So let me start off with Mr. Wilson if I might and try to pose the question as to what you think Russia—[laughter]—will be doing in regards to the new opportunities in Ukraine. Congressman Hastings mentioned that the issues of stronger exchanges between the two countries, whether its students or else-wise, that I think many of us in the West thought the history between Russia and Ukraine would serve the East—would serve the West well in building a strong relationship with Ukraine.

But looking forward, it's going to be based upon a mutual interest going forward. And Russia certainly has the geographical advantage over the West in developing a closer tie with Ukraine. Now, again, I personally believe that the United States needs to develop a closer relationship with Russia, so this is not saying this in a hostile sense. But trying to figure out the policies for the United States—how should we anticipate Russia's response to the opportunities in Ukraine?

Mr. WILSON. That's right. I think you're absolutely right. Ukraine and Russia should be expected to have good relations. There's every expectation that that should be the case. I think Russia and Russian leadership have learned some lessons in Ukraine. In 2004, then-President Putin overplayed his hand with pretty an outright, overt endorsement of candidate Yanukovych at the time for President.

And I think that actually hurt Yanukovych in 2004 because it was heavy handed. And I think the Ukrainian people who are open and receptive to close ties with their northern neighbor saw this as an overt effort to manipulate their political process and didn't like that, responded to that.

I think it's been interesting to watch over time the way that Moscow has related to Ukraine. In some respects, it become somewhat disenchanted with Yanukovych as their candidate, if you will, made more of an effort to develop a relationship with Prime Minister—at the time—Prime Minister Timoshenko, but dug in a hard line against President Yushchenko.

And I think some of the approach that Russia took over the past years during President Yushchenko's tenure were actually quite dangerous. The letter that Medvedev sent to Ukraine, basically refusing to have an Ambassador until the President was gone, President Putin's challenging of Ukraine's sovereignty at the Bucharest summit, certain activities taking place in Crimea—were downright potentially dangerous, laid the seeds for a potentially dangerous future.

But I think Russia looks at the situation in their view, they think they've had a bit of a victory, but I think it is a tactical victory. In one respect, they've seen the defeat of the Orange Revolution leaders, especially Yushchenko. Remember, Yushchenko actually ran in this election.

If he had been a successful President, he could have had a second term and delivered on a vision which had very much irritated the Russians. He failed. He lost. Now, I don't think Russia had the reason for why he lost. I think he lost on his own merits. But Russia also sees themselves as having succeeded in pushing NATO off the agenda. I do think these are tactical victories because, I think, as Dan Russell began, the principles of the Orange Revolution were not defeated in this process.

So I think it's important to watch this relationship. If Russia tries to exert, if you will, its sphere of privileged interest and expect Ukraine to do things that are Russia's bidding, such as open up the extension of the Black Sea Fleet in Sevastopol, to move on recognition of South Ossetia and Abkhazia—those would be very disconcerting signs. I think, for the moment, we've seen President Yanukovych resisting that type of pressure. He's given a nod toward issue like elevating the status of Russian language in Ukraine but that's a fair issue to have debated with inside Ukraine's polity. And I think the important part of this from U.S. policy is that we need to help support Ukraine as an independent actor, as a sovereign actor.

And we need to be very clear that when we talked about a Russia reset policy, we need to articulate, just as powerfully, the other side of that—that we pursue cooperative relations with Russia but not at the expense of our values of our friend or our friends. And I think when we see or sense this type of pressure on Ukraine, we should work with our European partners to push back and to push back very clearly on Moscow.

Mr. CARDIN. I think your benchmarks are good ones for us to follow because I really do think it's too early to tell not only what Ukraine will do but what Russia will be doing——

Mr. WILSON. That's right.

Mr. CARDIN [continuing.] And how it impacts on U.S. interests. I think it's just something we need to deal with. And I think the energy issue is probably going to be one of the most fundamental. I mean, you raise a very good point about gas prices in Ukraine are unrealistically low, which is having a major impact on their economy because the government subsidizing so much of the cost of energy. And we're not sure what impact this has on market forces. And then put on top of that the interest, internationally, on dealing with global climate change and energy security issues within that region, it is a matter that Ukraine could play a very positive role but it requires reform.

And when you do reform, there're winners and losers. And the current—I'm sorry, Dr. Aslund, if I get involved, a little bit, in politics here but the business leaders' impact in government decisions in Ukraine is well known. So the question is, can they go forward with these market reforms in the energy sector, not just from the point of view of the impact it has on its economy but on its political structure. And will the international organizations have enough impact, IMF, et cetera, in the reform commission's recommendations and implementation. What is your assessment on that?

Mr. ASLUND. Thank you very much. This is exactly the question that I wanted to get because I think that this is the key issue. When the IMF makes an agreement, normally it requires certain prior actions, the natural prior action for the IMF to demand now is that gas prices should be increased domestically before the IMF concludes any agreement. We can discuss how much. My basic view is the faster, the better. And then you provide social compensation for those who are really suffering. Normally, the people are really suffering—they don't use much gas.

So it's not so much you have to pay—from a state point of view, you can save $3 out of $4 by raising the prices and giving full social compensation. And I think that the Ukrainian Government is ready for this because they realize that they can't play an old game for too long. And what we are gradually seeing is that these big businessmen, they prefer to be owners of enterprises rather than sit and play in arbitrage, play between low, controlled prices and the free, much higher prices. So I think that this is the time to make the push. And the IMF, the U.S. and the European Union are all highly aware of this. And I do hope that they will hold firm and get that done.

Mr. CARDIN. Thank you. One of you mentioned the fact that I didn't realize that Ukraine has a large coal reserve—which I wasn't aware of. Is there a concern that you might find an increase in the utilization of coal, which could also compromise, then, our global climate change issues and deals with security issues also, as far as the pipelines, et cetera, as part of the way that Ukraine responds to the IMF's desires? Is that on the table?

Mr. ASLUND. I don't think that we should be much worried in this regard. The coal price is half of what it should be and the big states are——

Mr. CARDIN. They're also subsidizing coal?

Mr. ASLUND. Yeah. And there're big subsidies to the coal mines. The coal mine owners say, we don't need any subsidies if the prices are free. So if you have higher coal prices, the consumption will go down. In Soviet times, Ukraine consumed 110 billion cubic meters of gas each year. Now, it's down to 50 billion cubic meters. So just let the market function and you will get the reduction. Ukraine was the most energy intensive economy in the world in Soviet times—even worse than Russia. So therefore, you have huge benefits to get and Ukraine has reduced its emissions enormously and they can do much more and should do much more for their own benefit.

Mr. CARDIN. Well, I thank both of you for your testimony. I think it gives us a yardstick to judge what is happening in Ukraine and it's very helpful for our Commission. I'm going to turn the gavel over to Chairman Hastings. I have a commitment on the Senate floor this morning in about 10 minutes. So to not to be disruptive, I'll give him the gavel and thank you again for your testimony.

Mr. HASTINGS. Thank you very much, Mr. Chairman. And I agree with you that our witnesses were very specific and left very little that needs to be asked. At the very same time, in listening to your testimony I had a couple of takeaways and, specifically, Mr. Wilson, when you commented about the thrust to have a Europe whole and free, and we hear about Ukraine but I think about so many other flashpoints. Two that come to mind most immediately are Bosnia and Kosovo that have, kind of, like dropped off of the radar screen in the minds of most policymakers and a lot of folk in the administration.

And in my judgment, those two areas still pose considerable problems. The global downturn took a heavy toll on a considerable number of the areas of the former Soviet Union. And nearby to all of this are those Central Asian countries that have been laboring under what would be classified as recessionary times for a very long time. And so when you say, Dr. Aslund, right, that this is a unique opportunity to move ahead, as you put it, I wonder how do you move ahead when you don't have any money?

And put bluntly, if you look at the role—and we seem to rely heavily upon the International Monetary Fund, perhaps it would help me—and I'll start with you, well, Dr. Aslund, if you would tell me how that works with Russia as a player? And going even further into that, what tax consequences exist for Ukraine's citizenry and just where would they all find a revenue stream and how would they? Corrupt business persons—and we use that term—I'm always fascinated how we in the United States form a list of corruption and somehow—and I understand how we do that but if I was in another country, and I was looking at what happened on Wall Street the last 20 years, I'd wonder about the United States telling me about corruption. And I really—that's a blunt statement but maybe ours is just organized corruption some kind of way or another.

I'm reminded of a story, people were telling me how bad organized crime was in south Florida—and this is 40 years ago—and at that time, I had been robbed face-to-face with a gun three times, my house had been broken into seven times, I had three cars stolen—two from church—[laughter]—and I said that I wasn't as worried about organized crime as I was disorganized crime—[laughter]—that was about to kill me. So and that's a real true story about my own life and when the Prime Minister so rightly said the other day, Prime Minister Azarov, that the debts that are owed to the population and, in this case, Mr. Yanukovych rightly, as I'm sure Mr. Yushchenko must have as well, said that we're going to take care of you.

Don't worry. We're going to be able to pay you. And then, evidently, Azarov had done his own auditing and learned that he doesn't have anything to pay them with. And so where do they go from here, Dr. Aslund? And then I'll come back, Mr. Wilson, to you on a couple of other matters. I hope there were a few questions in there aside from personal ruminations. [Laughter.]

Mr. ASLUND. Thank you very much, Mr. Chairman. Well, certainly, I will start with one saying, booms are times of corruption, depressions are times of moral rearmament. And therefore, I think, that the crisis now is good. We see the same thing in Ukraine as here. People tolerate corruption much less when the times are bad than when they are good.

Mr. HASTINGS. I hear you.

Mr. ASLUND. And therefore, they want to do something about it. One area that this is very striking is in the red tape of petty corruption in the bureaucracy. Here, there is a strong general sense now in Ukraine, that we must do something about it. And we have seen several countries in the former Soviet Union—in particular,

Georgia but also Azerbaijan and Kyrgyzstan—have cleaned this up. If they can clean it up, why shouldn't Ukraine be able to do that? Ukraine is today the 110th country in the world in terms of GDP per capita, according to the IMF statistics which is far too low with a generally educated labor force and two-thirds of young now get some kind of higher education.

So you can say that human capital is hardly anywhere worse used than in Ukraine. So the essential thing is just, free them and give them possibilities to work. That doesn't cost money. That saves you money—cutting down the bureaucracy. And that's also reason why it should be possible to do the gas reform now because the government has to listen to the IMF and this here is rather limited number of corrupt people who are trying to benefit from that. It's much more difficult to do that in bad times. But, essentially, taxes in Ukraine are already high. Tax collection is good, surprisingly. The problem is too big public expenditures. I've already talked about the gas subsidies—or energy subsidies more broadly.

The second is discretionary enterprise subsidies, which are—(inaudible). The third big area is the pension expenditures. Ukraine spends 16 percent of GDP—more than twice as much as this country—on public pensions, which makes no sense. It goes to people who retired in the '40s through various early pension schemes. Their retirement age for women is 55, for men, 60. It doesn't make sense. These people should continue their work and so pension reform is a politically difficult thing that needs to be done.

With regard to Russia, Russia has a positive attitude toward IMF support for Ukraine and was interested in getting IMF money for Ukraine also in December when the big Western countries said no. With regard to the tax system, not that much needs to be changed there. It's mainly unnecessary public expenditures that go to the corrupt that should be stopped. Thank you.

Mr. HASTINGS. Well, turning again just very briefly, to Russia, it would seem to me that what they have done by cutting off their gas resources last year to Ukraine was particularly brutal in the dead of winter. And second, Ukraine pays the highest prices for their supplies of all of the European countries. And so Russia, whether they come, they get money from the IMF or not, seems to be in a position of win-win. And let's put something here on the table. I was at the first election. And I read the words of Mr. Yushchenko and Ms. Tymoshenko and Mr. Yanukovych and others whose names I can't remember.

But I distinctly remember that Mr. Yanukovych, at that time, was much more inclined to work with Russia than he was with the United States. So is there an old Yushchenko and a new one? Is— Yanukovych, I mean. And that's troubling to me. Don't they have— Russia—a lot of leverage on what happens with the energy resources in Ukraine? And if you are talking oligarch to oligarch in the business world, then without knowing—and I don't know anybody in Ukraine that's a rich man or woman that is in this business and I don't know anybody in Russia that's a rich man or woman in that business—every time I'm in both the countries I hear about the oligarchs but I don't ever see any or meet any—but I'll bet you they meet.

And therein lies the rub. How do you get crooks to not be crooked when they're making a lot of money? And what role, Mr. Aslund, does the shadow economy play? When I'm down in the train system in Kyiv, I can see—just like if I walk over here in Anacostia—I can see that shadow economy at work. And I'm not decrying it. Americans don't quite understand that a large part of the underpinning of this country is a shadow economy and if it didn't exist, we'd be in worse shape than we are now. For some strange reason, folk don't seem to want to accept that. But you come go with me to Pentagon City and I'll show you people—today—that are buying expensive garments and perfume and what have you that don't have no job nowhere. And didn't get it from welfare either.

So it's a strange environment that we live in, in this world. I'm sorry. Perhaps, Dr. Aslund, not to keep you on the spot—put those in the catalogue and then come back and talk to me about it and I'll go to Mr. Wilson and maybe along in the same vein. When we talk about reliable partners in energy—how are you going to be a reliable partner when somebody else has all of this leverage over you? And let's put something else on the table. While there's an extraordinary Ukraine diaspora here in the United States and elsewhere in the world, there are more Russians in Crimea or Russian-sympathizing people in Crimea than all of the diaspora combined.

So while it may very well be true that Russia did not defeat Yushchenko, the turnout in Crimea suggest to me that Russia may have helped Yanukovych. We do it on the straight up, with nice words and narratives but there was some evidence and talk on the streets of Russia's influence in the last election. And I don't decry that. We have our nonprofit organizations that work in an effort to try and make a difference for human rights and transparency and all of the rule of law and those fine things that we say and the other people just put money on the ground and get it done. I don't know whether there's anything for you to respond to. I think you and I are in thorough agreement about people-to-people exchanges. But how about you, Dr. Wilson?

Mr. WILSON. Sir, I will certainly pick up on a few of those points. There are—I mean, Russian-speakers play a major role in Ukraine and Ukrainian politics. But these Russian-speakers are citizens of Ukraine and have loyalty to Ukraine and are part of building a future of Ukraine. If Ukraine is to succeed, it has to have a role where the Russian-speakers in the east feel a part of that future.

Mr. HASTINGS. Agree.

Mr. WILSON. That is one of the areas where Yanukovych can potentially make progress. The problem is when leaders in Moscow look to manipulate and use Russian-speaking populations to advance their own interests in other countries. That's dangerous. That's interfering in the internal affairs of Ukraine.

Mr. HASTINGS. And we see that in Lithuania and Latvia——

Mr. WILSON. That's right, that's right. And part of it——

Mr. HASTINGS [continuing.] Slovakia and Slovenia.

Mr. WILSON [continuing.] Is soft influence through the power of Russian language media. So many of these folks getting their media out of Moscow. And part of it's more concerning where there're reports of folks acquiring Russian passports that provide a bit more of a pretense. This was the pretense that the Russians used in South Ossetia, Abkhazia—the protection of Russian citizens there—which was, frankly, a fabricated pretense. And I think that's something to keep an eye on. You asked a little bit about Yanukovych's disposition. And I think in 2004, 2005, it was essentially fair to say he was a pro-Russian candidate. He was backed by the Kremlin in that election. I think it's a little bit more nuanced now. And I think he certainly has adopted a much softer position toward Russia. He wants to pursue positive relations.

But he hasn't turned his back on Europe. He has pressed back on a NATO agenda, very clearly so. And that obviously pleases many in Moscow. But I think once you become President of Ukraine, it's, kind of, nice to be President of an independent, sovereign country. And I would hope that this position of responsibility would make him think more about the benefits to Ukraine of an independent streak, of an independent decisionmaking process. So while I don't decry an effort to develop a manageable relationship with Moscow, I think it is important that there not be early concessions just for the sake of it.

Mr. HASTINGS. Yeah, on the people-to-people exchange kind of thing, obviously, an American President cannot do everything. But it would seem to me—the Vice President has visited Ukraine. But I'm wondering and if I were President of the United States, I certainly would invite Yanukovych to come to the United States. And I think that that would be, singularly, just a Presidential visit would be particularly important in these times.

I don't know whether the administration is thinking along those lines or whether anything is planned but I see all sorts of Presidents come through here and I guess because of involvement in Europe, I have the attitude that I do, but if you're going—when you talk about, now he's President and it's an important thing to be President, then you have to give him the feeling of being President. And what better way could that be expressed than to have him come for a visit with the United States? And I'll make that recommendation to the administration.

Mr. WILSON. That's absolutely right. I concur with that. And I think President Yanukovych has been to Brussels, he's been to Moscow and he's planning to visit Washington as part of the nuclear security summit which President Obama will host in April. That's good because it gets him here to Washington at an early stage. It's a bit of a distracted platform because there will be a lot of foreign leaders here at the time. So I think it's important to think about how to maximize the impact of that particular visit.

But then also, how to follow that up because he will be overshadowed by many other leaders. I don't want to downplay the importance of it, but the power of having Ukrainians come to Washington regularly, come to the United States regularly—but also, even more importantly, it is very important for the United States to be present in Ukraine. It would be terrific to see President Obama make a trip to Ukraine in his first term. We've had the Vice President there, we've had the national security advisor. Secretary Clinton would be a natural followup.

President Yanukovych and President Medvedev have already agreed to, I think, three more meetings this year. They're neighbors. That's natural. They're close. But it's important for us to re-

member that we do need to be in the game. And that requires—
that's why your trips, your frequent trips to Kyiv, have mattered
so much. We need to have senior Americans showing up in
Ukraine, engaging their interlocutors, keeping these issues on the
agenda, cajoling, pressing but also exchanging information,
strengthening the ties here because they will be having that on a
very frequent basis with their Russian allies.

Mr. HASTINGS. I hear you. Dr. Aslund, I left all those questions
out there but I'm sure you have lots of answers for those questions
and you'll have the last word for us.

Mr. ASLUND. Thank you very much. Were very good questions,
Mr. Chairman. If I start with Russia—of course, Russia has an interest in selling gas to Ukraine and now it's spoiling that market.
Until 2008, Ukraine was actually the biggest purchaser of Russian
gas in the quantity. Now, with energy saving, Ukraine could stop
importing gas within a few years. Russia should understand that
that is not in their interest. The biggest impact we see of Russian
business in Ukraine is direct investment.

The two biggest outside investors in Ukraine are Russian businessmen who were actually born in Ukraine but now live in Moscow. And I think that this is a normal thing and we are also seeing
that the people who invest in the worst depression are big Russian
businessmen, because they are used to handle risk and are not
afraid of it. In particular, the big Russian banks are now expanding
fast in Ukraine. How does one make crooks honest? First, it's much
better that they own companies because when they defend their
companies against criminal practices rather than extort from other
enterprises and second, it's good if they get integrated into the outside world.

The people who make initial public offerings selling their stocks
abroad, they clean up the companies first, they bring in international auditing companies and make the companies more transparent. One of the cleanest sectors is actually the banking sector
because 40 percent of the banks are now owned by foreign banks—
mainly European banks but also Citi runs a good bank in Ukraine.

About the shadow economy, I share your sympathy because the
shadow economy is to considerable extent small private plots. Each
Ukrainian family has a private plot. If they are doing badly, they
live on subsistence agriculture because they have enough land so
that they can live on the land if necessary. And this is a quite important social safety net which is the explanation why the social
crisis has not been worse in this very bad economic downturn.
Thank you.

Mr. HASTINGS. Right, all right. I thank you both so very much and also the previous witness. And I can assure you that at the Commission that we will keep our interest level high as we proceed and I will try to persuade many of my colleagues to visit more and engage more and try best to gain greater understanding. Thank you so very much.

Mr. ASLUND. Thank you.

Mr. WILSON. Thank you.

[Whereupon, at 11:28 a.m., the hearing was adjourned.]

APPENDICES

PREPARED STATEMENT OF HON. ALCEE L. HASTINGS, CO-CHAIRMAN, COMMISSION ON SECURITY AND COOPERATION IN EUROPE

Thank you, Mr. Chairman, for holding this important and timely hearing. I had the privilege to serve as the Deputy Head of the OSCE Parliamentary Assembly election mission to Ukraine during the first round, January 17th elections. Judging by my personal experience and those of my OSCE colleagues in both rounds, these elections were largely free and democratic. This does not mean they were perfect. There were some problems stemming largely from the inadequate and confusing electoral framework. So there is no doubt that these laws need fixing before the next elections.

The ultimate victors in this election are the Ukrainian people. This is not something we should take for granted—regardless of whether or not one liked the outcome. To some Western observers, this may seem odd, but the fact these election results were not pre-ordained is a success in itself. The fact that voters do not know who will win a race is a new and rare concept in the region and puts Ukraine in stark contrast with some of its neighbors.

The world was enamored with the 2004 Orange Revolution, which brought millions of Ukrainians into the streets to peacefully protest election fraud, corruption and lack of rule of law. Since then, Ukraine has developed an open and pluralistic political system and media freedoms have expanded. Although Ukraine has had good elections now for the last five years—and I've had the opportunity to lead or otherwise contribute to three OSCE election missions to Ukraine during that time—I can tell you that you need more than good elections to make a functioning democracy.

Unfortunately, despite the progress, Ukraine has also witnessed poor governance, destructive infighting and political instability—in part due to no clear delineation of powers between the offices of prime minister and president. President Yanukovych, along with the just-appointed Prime Minister, Mykola Azarov, will need to seriously address long-standing problems that undermine Ukraine's potential, including corruption and the lack of an independent judiciary, which is a key underpinning for the rule of law.

Ukraine's leadership also needs to reform and make more transparent the troubled energy sector as well as a plethora of issues involving Crimea, be it the Black Sea Fleet, Russian influence, or inter-ethnic challenges, especially the plight of the Crimean Tatars. Ukraine must vigorously fight hate crimes. Ukraine has been especially hard-hit by the global financial crisis. Unfulfilled promises of the Orange Revolution led to disappointment and cynicism in Ukraine, as well as frustration among Ukraine's supporters in the United States and Europe. Obviously, the Ukrainian leadership's work is cut out for them.

President Yanukovych desires to improve relations with Russia and is certainly more oriented in that direction than his predecessor, but I don't believe would cede Ukraine back to a bygone era, and judging from his initial statements and visits, he clearly sees integration into the European Union as a priority. At the same time, he appears to value the benefits of a continued, strong relationship with the United States.

The United States has a solid record of standing with the Ukrainian people over the decades in support of their struggle for freedom and democracy. I look forward to hearing from our witnesses as to how we can maintain and strengthen our partnership with Ukraine.

PREPARED STATEMENT OF DANIEL A. RUSSELL, DEPUTY ASSISTANT SECRETARY OF STATE FOR EUROPEAN AND EURASIAN AFFAIRS

Chairman Cardin, Co-Chairman Hastings, Members of the Commission: Thank you for the invitation to discuss Ukraine and its relations with the United States in the wake of presidential elections. Your timing could not be better, as Ukraine's new president took office last month and its new government was confirmed last week.

WHY UKRAINE MATTERS

Let me begin by making three basic points about Ukraine and the recent elections before sketching out our agenda for engagement. My first point should be obvious: Ukraine matters to the United States and it matters to Europe. Ukraine is one of Europe's largest states, roughly the size of France with 45 million people. It serves as a transit route though which nearly a quarter of Europe's gas imports flow, and it could become self sufficient in energy, were its natural resources to be fully developed. Ukraine has tremendous potential. It could become a net contributor to global food security; its rich black soil produced over one-quarter of the Soviet Union's agricultural output. Ukraine can also serve as an example in a critical region. It has shown leadership on the world stage, giving up its nuclear weapons to become a non-nuclear state and contributing to security and peacekeeping operations from the Balkans to Iraq. And Ukraine's highly educated workforce is probably now more connected with Europeans and Americans through business, travel and education than ever before. Cell phones outnumber Ukrainians; about one-quarter of the population is on-line; and Ukrainians are travelling abroad in record numbers.

My second point is about Ukraine's leadership in democracy in the region, a role aptly illustrated by the conduct of its presidential elections in January and February. Taken together, the two rounds of voting received an overwhelmingly positive assessment by international observers. Among those observers were Congressman Hastings and Helsinki Commission staff members, and I would like to recognize their contribution to the OSCE Parliamentary Assembly's election observer mission. The OSCE concluded that the presidential election showed significant progress over previous elections, and met most OSCE and Council of Europe commitments. The open, competitive election demonstrated respect for civil and political rights and offered voters a genuine choice among candidates representing diverse political viewpoints. Candidates were able to campaign freely, and the campaign period was generally calm and orderly. The U.S. Senate, in fact, recognized the progress represented by this election with its passage of Resolution 422.

My third point is that the 2010 presidential election may have been a defeat for the Orange Revolution's leaders, but not for the Orange Revolution. The peaceful expression of the political will of Ukrainian voters should be viewed as another step in strengthening democracy in Ukraine. Ukraine has undergone rapid—and, I would suggest—irreversible, democratic change, and Ukrainians should take pride in what they have achieved. During the presidential campaign, Ukraine's vibrant body politic and free press discussed and debated the poor governance and chronic political infighting that has plagued the country. Ukraine's economy contracted 15% in 2009, one of the worst economic performances in the world. Voters, with access to independent information and the candidates' views, made up their own minds and turned out—and turnout exceeded 65% in each roundvote out the incumbents.

The post-election transfer of power has been orderly. After the votes were counted and certified, President Yushchenko stepped down and Viktor Yanukovych took the oath of office in the parliament as Ukraine's fourth president since independence. Prime Minister Tymoshenko initially challenged the results in court but later withdrew her case. She left office after a vote of no-confidence and President Yanukovych set about assembling a parliamentary majority coalition. When formation of a coalition appeared unlikely, threatening stalemate or early elections, Yanukovych and his Party of Regions sought and won passage of a new law that allows coalition formation based on votes not only of political parties but also independent deputies. On that basis, Prime Minister Mykola Azarov and his cabinet were confirmed last week. The opposition questioned the new law's constitutionality. We were pleased to see that the Party of Regions itself took the initiative to ask the Constitutional Court to review the law and pledged to abide by the court's decision. If the court rules against the new procedure, we expect the Party of Regions will seek to form a new coalition consistent with whatever the Court decides or seek early parliamentary elections.

Ukraine's democracy is a work in progress. The electoral process is contentious but as Vice President Biden told a Ukrainian audience when we visited Kyiv last July: "to those cynics who have asserted for centuries that this part of the world could never practice democracy because its culture and values are different, Ukraine today stands as resolute rebuttal . . ."

With the election behind him, President Yanukovych now faces the challenge of governing. Obviously, he and his new team need time to organize themselves and put policies and programs in place, but some key elements of his approach are already obvious. Economy recovery will rightly be the Yanukovych Presidency's top priority, and he has inherited a difficult situation at a difficult moment. Sound leadership and tough measures will be needed if he is to succeed. With regard to foreign policy, President Yanukovych has been quite clear. He says he wants to continue Ukraine's strategic partnership with the United States, improve relations with Russia, and pursue integration with the European Union. President Yanukovych made his first trip abroad to Brussels, his second to Moscow, and he has been invited to Washington to attend the President's Nuclear Security Summit in April. Let me add that the United States enjoyed a productive working relationship with Ukraine and with Mr. Yanukovych during his two previous tenures as prime minister.

U.S.-UKRAINE STRATEGIC PARTNERSHIP

As we look ahead to engagement with President Yanukovych and his new team, it is worth reviewing the underlying premises of our U.S. policy toward Ukraine. Simply put, the United States will not waiver in its support for a strong and independent Ukraine. We want to see Ukraine succeed; our vision for Ukraine is the vision Ukrainians have for themselves—a democratic and prosperous European nation with an effective and accountable government. Charting the course for Ukraine is, of course, a decision to be made by Ukrainians and their elected leaders. President Obama, in his speech in Moscow last July said, and I quote, "State sovereignty must be a cornerstone of international order. Just as all states should have the right to choose their leaders, states must have the right to borders that are secure, and to their own foreign policies. Any system that cedes those rights will lead to anarchy. That is why this principle must apply to all nations, including . . . Ukraine . . . ."

There has been speculation over the past year that the Obama Administration's efforts to improve ties with Russia would somehow threaten our relationship with Ukraine. This was not and is not correct. As we reset relations with Russia, we have reaffirmed our commitment to the sovereignty and territorial integrity of Ukraine and its neighbors. We do not believe that a partnership with one country must come at the expense of another. The United States, in fact, joined Russia last December in re-affirming the security assurances provided Ukraine in the 1994 Budapest Memorandum. Our larger goal is to encourage the transition to a multipartner world, in which like-minded nations can make common cause on our common concerns—the stronger our partners, the more effective our partnerships. A strong and independent Ukraine is good for Russia, good for the region and good for the world.

There also has been speculation about Ukraine's relationship with NATO during a Yanukovych presidency. Let me be clear that the United States continues to support Ukraine's deepening ties to NATO and to the European Union. But again, these are decisions to be made by Ukrainians and their elected leaders. We recognize that how far and how fast to proceed will be a Ukrainian choice.

President Yanukovych has said that he would continue programs of cooperation with NATO at existing levels but NATO membership was not on his agenda. We respect that choice and want Ukrainians to know that NATO's door remains open.

Because of the importance that we attach to our relationship with Ukraine, once the Central Election Commission had announced the full electronic results of the presidential election, President Obama was among the first world leaders to congratulate Viktor Yanukovych on his victory. The President wished Mr. Yanukovych success in carrying out his mandate and commended the Ukrainian people on the conduct of the vote. National Security Advisor General Jones subsequently led the U.S. delegation to the presidential inauguration, where he had a chance to meet not only with Ukraine's newly elected President, but Prime Minister Tymoshenko. Mrs. Tymoshenko will be one of the leaders of the opposition in parliament and we will continue our longstanding relationship with her in that new role. We also plan to work closely with leaders on the political scene, among them Member of Parliament Arseniy Yatsenyuk and Deputy Prime Minister Sergey Tigipko. The development of new democratic leaders is important for all parties in Ukraine.

Let me underscore that U.S. policy toward Ukraine will continue to focus on strengthening the strategic partnership between our two countries. The specifics of our engagement and cooperation with Ukraine will continue to be guided by the U.S.-Ukraine Charter on Strategic Partnership. The charter highlights the importance of our bilateral relationship and outlines enhanced cooperation across a broad spectrum of mutual priorities including economics, trade and energy; defense and security; strengthening democracy; and people-to-people and cultural exchanges. During Vice President Biden's trip to Kyiv last July, the U.S.-Ukraine Strategic Partnership Commission was established in order to advance the objectives of the charter. The commission now includes six autonomous working groups and met in Washington in December. We look forward to its next session in Kyiv.

Our commitment to Ukraine is evidenced by our assistance program—$123 million in FY2010. The goals of our assistance are to bolster peace and security, strengthen democratic institutions, promote economic growth and energy efficiency, enhance security and non-proliferation, secure Chernobyl, fight AIDS and HIV, and improve child health.

U.S. POLICY PRIORITIES

In the spirit of our strategic partnership with Ukraine, I would like to suggest five policy priorities, beyond traditional foreign policy cooperation, that should be high on our shared agenda with the Yanukovych Presidency:

First, the United States is committed to policies that contribute to a democratic and prosperous Ukraine and stands ready to help Ukraine reach agreement with the International Monetary Fund as soon as possible. The path to recovery and renewed prosperity runs through the IMF, which can help offer Ukraine a way out of the current crisis and open the door to lending from other international financial institutions and the European Union. That will require resolute leadership and hard decisions to undertake the critical reforms needed to cut the budget deficit, revive the banking system and phase out energy subsidies.

A second equally important policy area for Ukraine's long-term prosperity and economic freedom is energy sector reform. A gas sector based on transparency, competition, realistic pricing, and more energy-efficient gas distribution and consumption will be key, and the United States is coordinating closely with the European Union on this issue. Ukraine uses energy three times less efficiently than the EU average; the country consumes 50-60% more gas than it should. The United States is helping with a three-year pilot program designed to increase energy conservation and efficiency at the municipal level.

Third, the United States is ready to work to strengthen the business side of U.S.-Ukraine relations, which is weaker than we would like it to be. The United States remains Ukraine's 8th largest foreign investor, with $1.4 billion in foreign direct investment. We welcome President Yanukovych's remarks in favor of creating incentives for investors, such as lowering taxes and reducing red tape. Our business community tells us that much remains to be done to make Ukraine more attractive to investors, from tax code reform to increased transparency, from greater rule of law protection to serious action against corruption. The payment of VAT refunds would be a big step forward. One area where the U.S. private sector could do more is in Ukraine's nuclear power industry.

A fourth area of cooperation lies in nuclear security. The United States and Ukraine must continue to work together to reduce the threat of the spread of nuclear materials and technology to dangerous regimes or terrorist groups, while safeguarding the peaceful uses of nuclear energy. We look forward to building on our successful record on non-proliferation at the upcoming Nuclear Security Summit. Thanks to the leadership of Senator Lugar and former Senator Nunn, we can point to vital cooperation between Ukraine and the United States that has made the world safer. We recognize Ukraine's importance as a partner in the Global Initiative to Combat Nuclear Terrorism, which brings our experience and expertise together with those of over 70 other countries to fight nuclear terrorism.

Finally, the United States wishes to strengthen bilateral security and defense cooperation, which is an essential component of our strategic partnership. We are grateful to Ukraine for its contributions to international security. As part of this effort, we hope that Ukrainian parliament will pass legislation to allow joint military exercises on its territory this year in order to facilitate mutually beneficial military training activities. With regard to NATO, we look forward to cooperating with Ukraine to meet its objectives in the NATO-Ukraine Commission and in its Annual National Program, regardless of Ukraine's intentions regarding membership.

CONCLUSION

While the challenges in U.S.-Ukrainian relations are complex and demanding, I remain optimistic about the possibilities before us. It is important to both nations and both peoples to get U.S.-Ukraine relations right. We have a chance, at the beginning of a new presidency in Kyiv, to redouble our efforts. Let's ensure that Ukrainians and Americans, both in and outside of government, make the most of that chance.

Thank you. And I will be happy to answer your questions.

PREPARED STATEMENT OF DAMON WILSON, VICE PRESIDENT AND DIRECTOR OF THE INTERNATIONAL SECURITY PROGRAM, ATLANTIC COUNCIL

Mister Chairman, Mister Co-Chairman, Members of the Commission, I am honored to speak before you today about our relationship with Ukraine.

My perspective on Ukraine stems from years observing and developing U.S. policy toward Ukraine. Most relevant to this hearing, I served as Special Assistant to the President and Senior Director for European Affairs at the National Security Council in the run-up to the NATO Bucharest Summit during which the Alliance debated a Membership Action Plan for Ukraine. I also served as the NSC Director for Central, Eastern and Northern European Affairs, responsible for coordinating policy toward Ukraine in advance of the 2004 presidential election, during the Orange Revolution and during the first years of the Yushchenko presidency. My prior experience with Ukraine related to my work at NATO, where I served as Deputy Director of the Private Office of Secretary General Lord Robertson, as well as my work on NATO policy within the Department of State. I continue to follow Ukraine at the Atlantic Council.

Today, I would like to underscore why the issue of Ukraine should matter in Washington, outline some key benchmarks against which to judge the foreign and security policy of Ukraine's new president and government, and offer some recommendations for U.S. policy.

PROGRESS YET DISAPPOINTMENT

I believe it is important to begin our discussion by stressing that we should not underestimate what has happened in Ukraine this year. On January 17, Ukrainian authorities conducted a successful first round of the presidential election. Three weeks later, there was a very close run-off. Nearly 70% of Ukrainian voters turned out for each round. Domestic and international observers validated that the election met key standards. Protests were lodged using legal procedures. On February 25, a peaceful transfer of power occurred.

This election is a victory for the consolidation of democracy in Ukraine (even if the maneuvers in the Rada required to bring a Regions-led government to office stretched parliamentary practice).

Nonetheless, many of Ukraine's greatest supporters, including myself, remain disappointed. Why?

First, a good election does not necessarily translate into good governance. While Ukrainians have developed a track record on free and fair elections, their representatives have not yet demonstrated a track record of performance—a dynamic which over time risks undermining support for democracy in Ukraine.

Second, many observers are disappointed because we were buoyed by the vision Orange Revolution leaders offered of a democratic, free-market Ukraine firmly anchored in the West. We believed that there was a genuine opportunity to ensure that this vision was not just a long-term goal, but a realistic prospect. As Ukraine's partners, we responded rapidly to help consolidate this vision by acting to lift Jackson-Vanik restrictions, provide Market

Economy Status, conclude World Trade Organization (WTO) negotiations, offer a Millennium Challenge Compact to combat corruption, and support closer ties to both NATO and the European Union (EU). And yet President Yushchenko and successive Ukrainian governments were not in a position to deliver on their end because of their own infighting and the refusal in some cases to confront entrenched interests and battle corruption. A key window of opportunity closed.

Third, we are disappointed because of the timidity in the West to continue to support Ukraine. Indeed, at best, there is much talk of Ukraine fatigue. At worst, there is a growing acceptance that active support of Ukraine is considered provocative in Moscow.

President Yanukovych assumes the presidency in an atmosphere of pragmatism. And a sober assessment of Ukraine's prospects is appropriate. However, the vision of Ukraine in Europe remains important as it remains a motivator for tough policy decisions in Kyiv, as well as Brussels and Washington. We must not take this vision for granted. In the coming years, there is a good possibility that Ukraine will move further away rather than toward that vision. The most likely scenario is that Ukraine will muddle along.

WHAT IS AT STAKE?

Why does this matter? First, it matters for the quality of life of Ukrainian citizens. But it also matters geopolitically. In some sense, Ukraine is "untethered." Its future is not certain. Its future is being impacted by decisions being taken today. I do not want to exaggerate the situation, but it is potentially a dangerous period in Ukraine's history—an ancient nation, but a young state.

The history of conflict in Europe is about uncertainty in the space between Germany and Russia—that is the storyline of European history and war. This would not matter if the Russia of today had evolved and changed to become like the Germany of today. But Russia has not. Last September at the Atlantic Council, Senator Lugar warned against "slid[ing] into . . . a very ominous potential crisis" in Ukraine. He cautioned that "our inattention . . . could be disastrous."

This ancient nation of Ukraine just elected only its fourth president—its James Madison, if you will. Ukraine's statehood remains fragile. If Ukrainian democracy continues to succeed, and helps produce good governance and economic growth, it will serve as a powerful example in a region that desperately needs positive examples.

And that is why Russia has a strategy which is essentially rollback. This strategy is well articulated by Russia's leaders, including President Medvedev's declaration of "privileged interests," as well as in Russia's new Security Strategy. Neither the West nor Ukraine has a clear strategy.

BENCHMARKS FOR UKRAINE'S POLICY

Let me first address Ukrainian policy, as what President Yanukovych does will have more of an impact on Ukraine's place in the world than any outside actor. As we seek to evaluate the kind of partner we have in President Yanukovych, we should consider key issues, which essentially serve as a test for Ukrainian foreign policy.

- Russia. How does Kyiv manage its relations with Moscow? Many in the West are reassured by a Yanukovych presidency at it augurs a more stable, positive relationship with Moscow. But a stable and positive bilateral dynamic requires Ukraine to behave as and be treated as a sovereign, independent actor. Key issues on the agenda include whether Yanukovych maintains a non-recognition policy toward South Ossetia and Abkhazia and whether he opens the door to an extension of the Black Sea Fleet in Sevastopol.

- Energy Security. Russian interests have been keen to gain control of Ukraine's energy infrastructure. Yanukovych will have an opportunity to demonstrate whether he views energy as a national security issue or simply as a transactional issue. If he believes energy is a national security issue, the new government would pursue a serious energy efficiency strategy.

- International Economics. The government's handling of the International Monetary Fund will be an early test of its credibility. Similarly, does Yanukovych pursue the Russian proposal for a Common Economic Space in a way that negatively impacts Ukraine's WTO membership or prospects for a free trade agreement with the EU?

- Regional Relations. Does Ukraine use its regional weight to support the new pro-Western government in Moldova and adopt a constructive position regarding Transnistria? How Yanukovych handle ties with Belarusian leader Lukashenka and Georgian President Saakashvili will offer insights into the regional role Ukraine may play. Similarly, does Kyiv engage or neglect GUAM (which groups Georgia, Ukraine, Azerbaijan and Moldova) given Moscow's irritation with the organization?

- European Union. During the campaign, Yanukovych played up his support for Ukraine in the EU while downplaying NATO. In office, will he press hard to grow Ukraine's bilateral ties to the EU as well as take advantage of the Eastern Partnership? A free trade agreement and visa liberalization are practical steps which would help Ukrainians be Europeans and move the country toward Europe.

- Nonproliferation. Ukraine had a spotty nonproliferation record under then-Prime Minister Yanukovych. Will Ukraine's arms sales track record continue to improve given the economic interests at stake?

- NATO. NATO is clearly not at the top of the agenda. Nor should it be. But NATO-Ukraine relations do need to be on the agenda. Yanukovych in fact had a track record as prime minister of advancing NATO-Ukraine ties. So while the window has closed on rapid movement toward NATO, both sides should ensure there is substance to underpin the NATO-Ukraine Commission. As NATO is a demand-driven bureaucracy, the signals from Kyiv will determine the substance.

I would like to make a broader point about NATO. I believe it is an imperative to maintain the credibility of the historic Bucharest summit decision that Ukraine will become a member of the Alliance. If we look back in 5 to 10 years, and the Bucharest decision is seen as hollow, there will be damaging implications for the Alliance's credibility and for Ukraine. And on this point, Russia is not quiet; Russia's national security strategy commits it to undermining the Bucharest commitment.

In face of Russian opposition and genuine divisions within Ukraine, some have argued that we should aim for the "Finlandization" of Ukraine—independent, but not part of any alliance structure. While Finland is an exemplary partner of the Alliance and a possible future member, I believe the term Finlandization has no utility beyond the Cold War. When applied to Ukraine, analysts imply big powers taking decisions about Ukraine's future. I believe Ukraine must be in a position to determine its own future, including whether to pursue membership in any alliance.

These issues provide benchmarks against which we can judge the new government. I have modest expectations, but do believe Yanukovych can deliver on his campaign pledge to continue moving Ukraine toward Europe. Yet the most important factor to achieve this foreign policy goal is what the government does domestically. Yanukovych's reception in Western capitals will be determined by whether he governs effectively, protects democratic advances, stabilizes and grows the economy, and ensures Ukraine is a reliable energy partner.

IMPLICATIONS FOR U.S. POLICY

In the wake of the collapse of the Berlin Wall, "Europe whole, free and at peace" was not just a vision; it was a successful policy leading to the consolidation of democracy in Central and Eastern Europe and integration of the region into Europe's great institutions. This outcome was neither easy nor obvious.

The same bipartisan leadership demonstrated over the past 20 years is required today to "complete Europe"—that is, to finish the unfinished business of integrating the western Balkans and Eastern Europe into the European mainstream, including ultimately the European Union and NATO.

However, at present, we are missing the vision and the policy to extend this great success story to the south and east.

Russia has a strategy—unfortunately, one of rollback. The West does not yet have a coherent strategy, although Vice President Biden's trip to Kyiv last year helped lay out excellent broad principles for U.S. policy. We cannot afford to put Ukraine on the back burner or accept the argument that active U.S. engagement is somehow provocative toward Russia. We should not accept the argument that Ukraine is "messy" and too divided as an excuse not to engage. If so, we may lose Ukraine. Ukraine's future is in play today. While changes in Ukraine are unlikely to be decisive in the next few years, the trend lines could take Ukraine further away rather than closer to Europe. We do not want to look back at Ukraine's next election and wonder what happened.

Mister Chairman, as part of my effort to outline a way ahead for U.S. policy toward Ukraine, I offer six recommendations:

1. Be in the Game. The United States needs to be in the game. Ukraine is in play, and we need to engage and be present. The Obama Administration has sent a top-notch Ambassador, John Tefft, to Kyiv. The visits to Kyiv by Vice President Biden and Na-

tional Security Advisor Jones, as well as President Obama's early call to congratulate Yanukovych, are key steps in this effort. This high-level outreach should continue.

2. Articulate a Vision. We need to recommit to building a Europe whole and free, energizing the bipartisan tradition behind this vision and making clear that Ukraine has a place within this vision, as does Russia.

3. Maintain Funding. We need to protect our funding for transition in Ukraine, as the Freedom Support Act model of "graduation" no longer applies in Europe's East. Higher per capita GDP does not necessarily translate into a democratic Ukraine anchored securely in Europe.

4. Reach Beyond Leaders. Yushchenko was a failure. Yanukovych is unlikely to bring decisive change in Ukraine. We therefore need to ensure our relations with Ukraine extend beyond leaders. We should place emphasis on developing next generation leaders, engaging the regions, and fostering people-to-people ties. In this area, the European Union can lead given the prospect of visa-free travel.

5. Push Energy Efficiency. The United States and Ukraine need to get serious about working with European partners to support energy efficiency in Ukraine as a national security strategy.

6. Enhance Mil-Mil Ties. We must ensure that close military-to-military ties continue and are backed with funding through Foreign Military Financing and Foreign Military Sales. We should cultivate mil-mil links between Ukraine and NATO as well as with Allied nations. And we must push back when Russia tries to portray military cooperation with Ukraine as provocative.

In the wake of Ukraine's election, Yanukovych is now president and his party leads the government. Now is the time to move beyond stalemate. Just as much as we hold Kyiv to that standard, we must hold ourselves to that standard.

Thank you, Mister Chairman, Mister Co-Chairman, and Members of the Commission. I look forward to answering your questions.

[NOTE.—The views expressed in this testimony do not necessarily represent the views of the Atlantic Council.]

PREPARED STATEMENT OF ANDERS ÅSLUND, SENIOR FELLOW, PETERSON INSTITUTE FOR INTERNATIONAL ECONOMICS

Mr. Chairman,

I would like to thank you for this opportunity to speak on an important topic, will Ukraine move beyond stalemate in the sphere of economic reform. Geopolitically Ukraine is an important country that has still not found its space and its relations with the United States are entirely friendly.

Ukraine must be congratulated on having carried out a series of free and fair elections. The country has undergone no less than three democratic and peaceful presidential transfers of power in sharp contrast to other countries in the former Soviet Union. Since 2005 Freedom House has classified Ukraine as a free country.

UKRAINE'S PREDICAMENT

Ukraine has established an open market economy with predominant private ownership. From 2000 to 2007, the country enjoyed an average economic growth of 7.5 percent, but the global financial crisis hit it hard. The economic crisis has illuminated the malfunction of the Ukrainian state and economy. Last year, Ukraine's gross domestic product slumped by no less than 15 percent, one of the biggest plunges in the world. Economically, Ukraine is not performing up to its potential. In 2009, the International Monetary Fund (IMF) assessed that its GDP per capita will be as little as $2,540 in current US dollars, placing it 110th in the world.

Qualitative international comparisons present an even more worrisome picture. I its 2009 overview, the World Economic Forum ranked Ukraine 72nd among 131 countries. Ukraine is lagging behind most in three areas: institutions, macroeconomic stability, and goods market efficiency, while it is doing comparatively well with regard to education, labor market efficiency, and innovation. This impressive human capital does not produce as much as it could because the state malfunctions, not delivering macroeconomic stability while impeding the free operation of private enterprise.

According to the European Bank for Reconstruction and Development, Ukraine is a relative laggard among the post-Soviet countries in terms of economic and institutional reforms. A comparative World Bank study in 2005 assessed that Ukraine was one of the post-Soviet countries with the least amount of novel market economic legislation. Since then Ukraine has adopted minimum new legislation, while another laggard, Georgia, has forged ahead.

A more specialized international comparison, the World Bank Doing Business index, shockingly ranks Ukraine 142nd out of 183 countries by business environment. It is particularly arduous to obtain construction permits and carry out tax payments, but it is also difficult to start and close a business, to register property, and to trade across borders. Similarly, Transparency International ranks Ukraine 146th out of 180 countries on its 2009 corruption perception index.

Because of the many years of neglecting reform, tasks have in many ways become more difficult in Ukraine. First, legislation is substandard. The common statement that Ukraine has good laws but they have not been implemented is not true. On the contrary, the country has few modern laws, and the quality of new legislation is generally considered unsatisfactory. Too much Soviet legislation has persisted for too long, and it permeates many new laws. During the many years of distorted markets, multiple vested interests have twisted many laws to their advantage. Endemic corruption has bred legislation that offers corrupt officials the opportunity to reap more corrupt revenue. The competence to draft laws has also been insufficient.

Second, not only the legislation but also the legislative process is tilted to the advantage of vested interests. This process is inordinately complex and non-transparent in Ukraine. It should be opened up, abridged, and made more cohesive. It must be made easier for the ruling political forces to have legislation adopted in line with their design.

Third, the government's capacity to formulate and carry out reforms is limited. The great bureaucratization and centralization mean that central authorities are overwhelmed by decision making on all kinds of current matters, leaving them little time for reforms. Therefore, the Ministry of Finance or the Ministry of Economy can hardly lead reforms as has been the case in other countries.

On the other hand, because many other postcommunist countries have already undertaken the necessary reforms, Ukraine can learn from their successes and failures, which renders it an advantage to be a laggard.

A Window of Opportunity for Economic Reform

At present, Ukraine faces an extraordinary window of opportunity. The country has both a unique political possibility and great economic need to launch a new wave of reform that will lay the foundation for sustainable economic growth. The new Ukrainian authorities need to act fast and forcefully to shore up the state. A presidential election offers a great opportunity for a new start. The new president enjoys a political mandate and parliamentary majority. A new government has just been formed and is ready to govern. But the period of "extraordinary politics," when the parliament and public allow the president to act fast and radically, will probably be brief.

So far, Ukraine has experienced two waves of substantial reform. The first reform wave started in the last quarter of 1994, after Leonid Kuchma was elected president. The second wave arose in the first quarter of 2000, when Kuchma was reelected and Victor Yushchenko became prime minister. In these two cases, reforms occurred immediately after a presidential election and in the midst of financial and economic crisis, underlining that Ukraine currently has a great chance to reform. Today, Ukraine is once again in such a situation. It badly needs to launch a new wave of substantial and comprehensive reforms.

Seeing this situation arising last fall, I initiated and served as co-chairman of an Independent International Expert Commission on a reform program for Ukraine after the presidential elections together with Ukrainian colleagues. It was meant to be an action program for the first year of a new presidency. Our proposal was endorsed by Ukraine's prime minister last September and also the new administration has expressed its appreciation. Half of the commissioners we invited were Ukrainians and the other half foreigners. They were prominent experts on different aspects of reform and policy and independent of government, political parties, and business. The work of the Commission was financed by the Swedish and Netherlands Ministries for Foreign Affairs, with additional support from the United Nations Development Program. We have published our report "Proposals for Ukraine: 2010—Time For Reforms," and I would like to report to you our key findings.

REFORM PRIORITIES FOR UKRAINE IN 2010

Mr. Chairman,

The new presidential mandate, the shock of a recent severe economic crisis, and popular dissatisfaction with the status-quo create ideal conditions for successful reforms. Our three main conclusions are: Ukraine needs (1) new organizational capacity for reforms, and (2) clear prioritization of reforms, and (3) utilization of international organizations as lighthouses to guide its reforms.

Our Commission's first conclusion was that Ukraine needs to establish new capacity to carry out reforms that is independent of the agencies to be reformed. We recommend the creation of a Reform Commission at the Cabinet of Ministers, headed by a Deputy Prime Minister with overarching authority. The Reform Commission should have its own budget and a single goal: to design and implement reforms. Together with the European Integration Secretariat, it should lead Ukraine's reforms from the Cabinet of Ministers. President Yanukovych formed a Reform Committee at the Presidential Administration that he chairs himself on his second day in office. He has also appointed a Deputy Prime Minister for Economic Reform.

Our second conclusion was that Ukraine needs to formulate clear priorities for reforms. First things need to be done first. Ukraine must: (a) improve the effectiveness of the state, (b) achieve financial stability, (c) allow private enterprise freedom on the market, and (d) make social policy more effective. Our selection is based on experts' views of priorities that are also politically feasible within one year. The new government has adopted a coalition program called "Stability and Reform." To a considerable extent, it reflects the views of our commission as Ukraine benefits from a broad consensus on what needs to be done.

The problem in Ukraine has not been what to do but who should do it, as far too often policymaking ends up in gridlock. Our third conclusion is therefore that it is necessary for Ukraine to use its international leverage or external guidance to break through the domestic logjam on reforms. The Commission has identified three anchors that can guide Ukraine to realize its commitment to its reforms: The IMF, the European Union and the World Bank. All these organizations are ready to engage with the new Ukrainian administration. Naturally, the United States should also engage in the promotion of reforms beneficial for Ukraine's future governance and economic welfare.

In the view of our commission, Ukraine's ten top priorities for 2010 are:

1. Carry out gas reform!
2. Make the National Bank of Ukraine (NBU) independent!
3. Move toward inflation targeting!
4. Cut public expenditures!
5. Undertake comprehensive deregulation of enterprise!
6. Conclude a European Association Agreement!
7. Get privatization going again!
8. Legalize private sales of agricultural land!
9. Adopt a Law on Public Information!
10. Complete the modern commercial legislation!

All these measures have been chosen on the basis that they are truly vital and can be implemented within one year. Some of them are simple, such as the legalization of private sales of agricultural land and the adoption of a law on public information, while others require some explanation.

The top priority is to reform the gas sector. At present, Ukraine is actually subsidizing imported Russian gas to the tune of 3 percent of GDP a year. This must cease. The government needs to adopt a realistic energy pricing policy. All energy prices should be brought to the level of full cost recovery plus a profit margin for operators as soon as possible. The Cabinet of Ministers should develop and adopt a Concept for Liberalization of the Gas Market in Ukraine, which should lead to the adoption by parliament of a Law on Principles of the Natural Gas Market Functioning to establish the principles for the natural gas market so that it performs transparently and efficiently, and stimulate competition. In line with the EU-Ukraine Brussels Declaration on renovation of the Gas Transit System of March 2009, the government should develop a plan for renovation and modernization of the gas transit system and attract financing from interested international financial institutions. In parallel with the price hikes, the Cabinet of Ministers should introduce a new system of targeted social assistance for the least protected groups of consumers who suffer because of high gas, electricity, and coal prices. Gas reform must be an absolute condition for international assistance.

In order to secure macroeconomic stability, it is essential to minimize potential conflicts between the government and the NBU. The independence of the NBU needs to be reinforced and its governance improved, as it is currently seen as being unduly influenced by both commercial and political forces. The NBU Council, whose role is unclear and is dominated by prominent business representatives and politicians, should be abolished in its present form, while the NBU chairman and his/her deputies should be given fixed terms. The political authorities should refrain from enacting legislation that impinges on NBU independence, such as proposals to finance various government expenditures by advancing the payment of NBU profits. The Ukrainian monetary policy should instead be governed by an independent Monetary Policy Committee consisting of independent professionals with well-defined powers and fixed terms. The NBU should also raise its professional quality and include prominent international expertise. A new law on the NBU reflecting these elements should be drawn up and adopted.

Ukraine should move toward inflation targeting regime within the next three years, which presupposes a floating exchange rate.

The transition period should offer the NBU enough room to bring down inflation to the 2 to 3 percent range and provide guidance to the public on the future development of the exchange rate, as well as fostering a reduction of dollarization. In the meantime, the NBU should proceed expeditiously with streamlining its monetary policy instruments and its decision-making process.

Ukraine needs to balance the state budget in the medium term by cutting public expenditures. The government should reconsider the obligations of the state in order to make them financially affordable. The authorities should resist any expansionary fiscal initiatives. Three public expenditures stand out as excessive: price subsidies, enterprise subsidies, and pension expenditures. Price subsidies and enterprise subsidies should be minimized, while pension expenditures need to be brought under control through a profound pension reform. It appears both unrealistic and harmful to try to increase the level of state revenues in Ukraine.

An overall aim must be a major improvement of the business environment, which should entail the strengthening of the legal base and property rights. The state's interaction with private enterprises needs to be reduced and simplified. Starting a business currently requires ten procedures that take 27 days, according to the Doing Business in Ukraine report. This process should be reduced to one procedure: registration of the business with the tax authorities and receiving a taxpayer number. It should take only one day and cost nothing as is the case in New Zealand. A new law on the liquidation of enterprises is needed to minimize the time needed as well as the cost, while maximizing the recovery rate. The issuance of construction permits is exceedingly difficult in Ukraine. The goal should be to simplify the process from 30 procedures to a small fraction and reduce the time required from 476 days to a small fraction. Procedures for registering property can be reduced from ten to probably three. The list of economic activities subject to mandatory licensing should be minimized to only those that are dangerous to human health and life, environment, or national security. A new Law on Licensing should establish firm legal limits of licensing. The requirement of official permits should be reviewed and limited to an exclusive list of economic activities, which should be sanctified by law. The government should sharply reduce the number of agencies entitled to undertake inspections as well as slash the number of legitimate reasons for inspections to the safeguarding life and health.

All these measures can be implemented within one year. The IMF will play a central role in implementing the gas reform and the macroeconomic policies in return for a two-year standby agreement with substantial financing. The European Union is currently negotiating a substantial association agreement including a comprehensive and deep free trade agreement. The EU is also deeply involved in the gas reform.

The United States plays a key role in the IMF as its biggest shareholder, and it should also engage in the gas reform which will be crucial not only for state finances and energy efficiency but also for the improvement of governance in Ukraine. The United States has a major interest in the economic success of a democratic and friendly Ukraine.

MATERIAL SUBMITTED FOR THE RECORD BY HIS EXCEL-LENCY OLEH SHAMSHUR, AMBASSADOR OF UKRAINE TO THE UNITED STATES OF AMERICA

Dear Chairman Cardin,

Dear Co-chairman Hastings,

Distinguished Members of the Commission

Let me start with expressing appreciation of the very important work that is being done by the US Congress Commission on Security and Cooperation in Europe. We value your consistent support of Ukraine in her efforts to pursue the path of democratic reforms and play an active role as contributor to regional and European security.

Ukrainian presidential election that took place earlier this year should be viewed within the context of the developments that had been taking place in this country since 2005. In spite of considerable political turbulence and recent acute economic problems, this period has been characterized by further development of democratic institutions, strengthening civil society and freedom of speech, emergence of the political culture free from intimidation and harassment of opponents.

Thus, Ukraine has made substantial gains in her democratic evolution. It was this environment and Ukrainian people's strong commitment to democracy that enabled the conduct of free and transparent parliamentary elections in 2006 and 2007 as well as the last Presidential election. H. Tagliavini, Head of the OSCE ODIHR observation mission concluded that this was "a well-administered and truly competitive election offering voters a clear choice". We highly appreciate the fact that Co-chairman Hastings visited Ukraine as a Deputy Head of the OSCE Parliamentary Assembly election observation mission.

New President and a newly formed Government of Ukraine are facing a number of serious challenges. First and foremost they are related to the pressing need to overcome the consequences of the crisis that has hit Ukrainian economy. It is quite clear that this goal cannot be achieved without a series of immediate steps (the Government has already started the work on the new, realistic budget) and systemic reforms aimed at rehabilitation and improvement of national finances, overhaul of the energy sector, including the emphasis on energy saving and energy efficiency, large-scale modernization of Ukraine's industrial base following innovation model of development, amelioration of investment climate, reduction of fiscal pressure.

President Yanukovych stated his determination to carry out structural economic reforms and get Ukrainian economy firmly back on track. He called for the diminishing of the Government's interference into economy and introduction of clear and constant rules governing relationship between the State and the private sector, reforms of pension and health care systems. By one of his first decrees he has established the Committee on Economic Reforms. It will serve as an advisory body to the President focusing on devising the overall reform strategy and the most urgent economic measures, elaboration of the corresponding implementation mechanisms.

The President and the Government have also indicated their willingness to resume active cooperation with all international financial institutions, including IMF in the framework of the stand-by arrangement for Ukraine.

Another set of pressing problems is defined by the need to improve the system of governance, eliminate causes of frequent conflicts between different branches of power that have led to the political gridlock. In his inaugural speech new President of Ukraine stressed that ensuring domestic stability and overcoming corruption were at the top of his policy priorities list. Both objectives cannot be achieved without reforming the system of state management and raising its efficiency, that include constitutional and judicial reforms, ensuring true independence of the judiciary.

In the field of foreign policy, during his meetings in Brussels with EU leadership President Yanukovych underscored that European integration is a key goal for Ukraine. He believes that the policy of European integration provides Ukraine with a strategy of societal reforms, and as such it can become a powerful factor uniting all Ukrainians.

Main efforts of Ukrainian diplomacy in relations with the European Union are now concentrated on finalizing negotiations process on the agreement on association and creation of the free trade area, introduction of the visa-free regime and cooperation in mitigating the consequences of the financial and economic crisis in Ukraine.

It should be noted that creation of a comprehensive free-trade area will enable Ukraine's gradual integration into the EU internal market and open up new investment opportunities for the European business in Ukraine, while Association Agreement as a whole will mark a qualitative step forward in Ukraine's cooperation with European institutions. Ukraine is also ready for the constructive interaction with the European Union through the EU's Eastern Partnership initiative.

In our quest for European integration we have been encouraged by the recent resolution of the European Parliament that for the first time has recognized that "Ukraine is a European state and, pursuant to Article 49 of the Treaty on European Union, may apply for membership of the EU like any European state that adheres to the principles of liberty, democracy, respect for human rights and fundamental freedoms, and the rule of law".

Substantial attention of the new state leadership will be drawn to the development of friendly, mutually beneficial and pragmatic relations between Ukraine and the Russian Federation in all spheres, including the sphere of energy. Ukraine will tackle energy issues proceeding from her possibilities and national interests.

There is no doubt that relations with the United States will remain in the centre of the foreign policy of Ukraine. In the course of the telephone conversation of 11 February 2010 Presidents Yanukovych and Obama confirmed their mutual willingness to promote further development of Ukraine-USA relations on the basis of the Charter on Strategic Partnership. Signed in December 2008 the Charter states the intention of our nations to deepen our partnership and expand our cooperation across a broad spectrum of mutual priorities in the economic, political, diplomatic, cultural, and security fields. We are proud that our partnership is a relationship of two democracies based on shared values and interests.

Ukraine is ready to enhance positive dynamic acquired by bi-lateral cooperation in the course of the previous period. First of all, we are looking forward to intensification of our political dialogue, especially to organizing the meeting at the highest level. We also expect productive outcome from the forthcoming sessions of the major bilateral bodies—Commission on Strategic Partnership, Working Groups on energy security, non-proliferation and export control, science, technology and education, consular issues, Defense Consultations and Council on Trade and Investment. We hope that they will widen the scope of practical, mutually advantageous projects to be implemented by our two countries.

Ukraine, having voluntarily relinquished the third largest nuclear arsenal in the world, continues to play a constructive role in safeguarding global non-proliferation regime. Let me use this opportunity to reiterate our support for the US efforts in the field. We share the goals of the Prague initiative of President Obama, and will continue to work together with the USA and other nations to make future Nuclear Security Summit in Washington a success.

○

This is an official publication of the
**Commission on Security and
Cooperation in Europe.**

This publication is intended to document
developments and trends in participating
States of the Organization for Security
and Cooperation in Europe (OSCE).

All Commission publications may be freely
reproduced, in any form, with appropriate
credit. The Commission encourages
the widest possible dissemination
of its publications.

http://www.csce.gov

The Commission's Web site provides
access to the latest press releases
and reports, as well as hearings and
briefings. Using the Commission's electronic
subscription service, readers are able
to receive press releases, articles,
and other materials by topic or countries
of particular interest.

Please subscribe today.

www.ingramcontent.com/pod-product-compliance
Lightning Source LLC
Chambersburg PA
CBHW081121280526

45787CB00007B/2929